Epworth Com

Gene
Ivor

The Pastor

Epworth Commentaries

Already published

The Book of Job
C. S. Rodd

Isaiah 1–39
David Stacey

The Books of Amos and Hosea
Harry Mowvley

The Gospel of Matthew
Ivor H. Jones

The Gospel of John
Kenneth Grayston

The First Epistle to the Corinthians
Nigel Watson

The Second Epistle to the Corinthians
Nigel Watson

The Epistle to the Galatians
John Ziesler

The Epistle to the Philippians
Howard Marshall

The Epistle to the Colossians
Roy Yates

The Epistle to the Hebrews
Paul Ellingworth

The Epistle of James
Michael J. Townsend

The Johannine Epistles
William Loader

Revelation
Christopher Rowland

In preparation

The Book of Ezekiel
Charles R. Biggs

I and II Thessalonians
Neil Richardson

THE
PASTORAL EPISTLES

I and II Timothy
and
Titus

MARGARET DAVIES

EPWORTH PRESS

ISBN 0 7162 0504 1

First Published 1996
by Epworth Press
1 Central Buildings Westminster
London SW1H 9NR

Typeset by Regent Typesetting, London
Printed and bound in Great Britain by
Biddles Ltd, Guildford and King's Lynn

For Peter, Gloria, John and Sheila.

CONTENTS

Contents

II TIMOTHY

TITUS

GENERAL INTRODUCTION

The *Epworth Preachers's Commentaries* that Greville P. Lewis edited so successfully in the 1950s and 1960s having now served their turn, the Epworth Press has commissioned a team of distinguished academics who are also preachers and teachers to create a new series of commentaries that will serve the 1990s and beyond. We have seized the opportunity offered by the publication in 1989 of the Revised English Bible to use this very readable and scholarly version as the basis of our commentaries, and we are grateful to the Oxford and Cambridge University Presses for the requisite licence. Our authors will nevertheless be free to cite and discuss other translations wherever they think that these will illuminate the original text.

Just as the books that make up the Bible differ in their provenance and purpose, so our authors will necessarily differ in the structure and bearing of their commentaries. But they will all strive to get as close as possible to the intention of the original writers, expounding their texts in the light of the place, time, circumstances, and culture that gave them birth, and showing why each work was received by Jews and Christians into their respective Canons of Holy Scripture. They will seek to make full use of the dramatic advance in biblical scholarship world-wide but at the same time to explain technical terms in the language of the common reader, and to suggest ways in which Scripture can help towards the living of a Christian life today. They will endeavour to produce commentaries that can be used with confidence in ecumenical, multiracial, and multifaith situations, and not by scholars only but by preachers, teachers, students, church members, and anyone who wants to improve his or her understanding of the Bible.

Ivor H. Jones

PREFACE

Readers can expect from this commentary an exploration and eluci-
dation of the theological and christological ethics of the Pastoral
Epistles, I and II Timothy and Titus. In writing it, I have drawn on
the insights of many other commentaries and studies, and have tried
to learn from them even while disagreeing with some details.
Alternative and disputed interpretations will be mentioned in the
general comment, but technical questions, especially those about the
language and style of the Pastorals, will follow in the notes, so that
readers can pursue them if they wish. At the end of the commentary,
readers will find a short essay about the possible authorship of the
epistles.

The Epworth Commentaries assume that readers will have before
them the Revised English Bible, 1989, and this commentary will
quote in italics from that version. The REB seeks to convey the sense
of the Greek in an English style which is both intelligible and
elegant. But all translations are interpretations, and the commentary
will point out when paraphrase has obscured alternative possible
meanings. Footnotes will be avoided, but when reference is made to
other scholarly studies, names and dates will appear in brackets, and
further particulars can be found in the bibliography.

Within the limited compass of this commentary, some attention
will be given to possible contemporary responses to these ancient
epistles' teachings. It may be helpful, therefore, if I forewarn readers
about my own commitments, which will inevitably colour my read-
ings. I am a female university teacher, a socialist who is committed
to civil liberties, and a member of the Anglican church. I shall try to
do justice to the epistles' insights within the cultural and historical
context in which they first appeared, but I shall admit that sometimes I would have preferred the epistles to express different views.

I am very grateful for the patient care and useful suggestions of
Miss Jean Cunningham at SCM Press.

Margaret Davies
Sheffield University

ABBREVIATIONS

BCE	Before the Common Era
BJRL	*Bulletin of the John Rylands Library*, Manchester
BZ	*Biblische Zeitschrift*, Paderborn
CBQ	*Catholic Biblical Quarterly*, Washington, D.C.
CD	The Covenant of Damascus, one of the Dead Sea Scrolls
CE	The Common Era
Diog. L.	Diogenes Laertius
ET	English translation
ICC	International Critical Commentary
JBL	*Journal of Biblical Literature*, Philadelphia
Josephus, *Ant.*	Josephus, *Antiquities of the Jews*
JSNT	*Journal for the Study of the New Testament*, Sheffield
JSNT SS	JSNT Supplement Series
JTS	*Journal of Theological Studies*, Oxford
LXX	The Septuagint, the Greek translation of the Hebrew Scriptures, which includes those books placed in the Apocrypha in some modern versions of the Bible
NovT	*Novum Testamentum*, Leiden
NT	New Testament
NTS	*New Testament Studies*, Cambridge
Plutarch, *Mor.*	Plutarch, *Moralia*
REB	Revised English Bible
SBL DS	Society of Biblical Literature, Dissertation Series
SNTS	Studiorum Novi Testamenti Societas

BIBLIOGRAPHY

Recent Commentaries

Dibelius M., and Conzelmann H., *The Pastoral Epistles*, edited by H. Koester, ET, Hermeneia, Philadephia: Fortress, 1972.

Fee, G. D., *1 and 2 Timothy and Titus*, A Good News Commentary, San Francisco: Harper and Row, 1984.

Guthrie, D., *The Pastoral Epistles. An Introduction and Commentary*, Tyndale NT Commentaries, Grand Rapids: Eerdmans, Leicester: IVP, 1957.

Hanson, A. T., *The Pastoral Epistles*, New Century Bible, Grand Rapids: Eerdmans, London: Marshall, Morgan and Scott, 1982.

Houlden, J. L., *The Pastoral Epistles*, The Pelican NT Commentaries, Harmondsworth: Penguin, 1976.

Karris, R. J., *The Pastoral Epistles*, NT Message 17, Wilmington: Michael Glazier, 1979.

Kelly, J. N. D., *A Commentary on the Pastoral Epistles*, Black's NT Commentaries, London: A. and C. Black, New York: Harper, 1963.

Knight, G. W., *Commentary on the Pastoral Epistles* New International Greek NT Commentary, Grand Rapids: Eerdmans, 1992.

Recent Studies

Davies, M., *The Pastoral Epistles*, NT Guide, Sheffield: Sheffield Academic Press, forthcoming.

Donelson, L. R., *Pseudepigraphy and Ethical Argument in the Pastoral Epistles*, Tübingen: J. C. B. Mohr, P. Siebeck, 1986.

B. Fiore *The Function of Personal Example in the Socratic and Pastoral Epistles* Analecta Biblica 105, Rome: Biblical Institute, 1986.

Kidd, R. M., *Wealth and Beneficence in the Pastoral Epistles*, SBL DS 122, Atlanta: Scholars Press, 1990.

MacDonald, M. Y., *The Pauline Churches: A Socio-historical study of Institutionalization in the Pauline and Deutero-Pauline Writings*, SNTS Monograph Series 60, Cambridge: CUP, 1988.

Verner, D. C., *The Household of God: The Social World of the Pastoral Epistles*, SBL DS 71, Chico: Scholars Press, 1983.

Young, F., *The Theology of the Pastoral Epistles*, NT Theology, Cambridge: CUP. 1994.

Other works cited

Barrett, C. K., *The Pastoral Epistles*, Oxford: Clarendon, 1963.

Brox, N., 'Zu den personlichen Notizen des Pastoralbriefe', *BZ* 13, 1969, pp. 76-94.

Campbell, R. A., *The Elders. Seniority within Early Christianity*, Edinburgh: T. and T. Clark, 1994.

— 'Identifying the Faithful Sayings in the Pastoral Epistles', *JSNT* 54, 1994, pp. 73-86.

Campenhausen, H. von, *Ecclesiastical Authority and Spiritual Power in the Church of the First Three Centuries*, ET London: A. and C. Black 1969.

Colson, F. H., 'Myths and Genealogies. A note on the polemic of the Pastoral Epistles', *JTS* 19, 1917-18, pp. 265-271.

Cook, D., 'The Pastoral Fragments Reconsidered', *JTS* NS 35, 1984, pp. 120-131.

Ellis, E. Earle, 'Pseudonymity and Canonicity of NT Documents', in M. J. Wilkins and T. Paige (eds.) *Worship, Theology and Ministry in the Early Church. Essays in Honor of Ralph P. Martin*, JSNT SS 87, Sheffield, Sheffield Academic Press, 1992, pp. 212-224.

Harrison, P. N., *The Problem of the Pastoral Epistles* Oxford: OUP, 1921.

— *Paulines and Pastorals* London: Villiers, 1964.

Hennecke, E., *New Testament Apocrypha* edited by W. Schneemelcher, ET 2 vols. London, Lutterworth, 1963, 1965, London: SCM Press, 1973, 1974.

Hitchcock, F. R. Montgomery, 'Philo and the Pastorals', *Hermathena* 56, 1940, pp.113-135.

Horrell, D., 'Converging Ideologies: Berger and Luckmann and the Pastoral Epistles', *JSNT* 50, 1993, pp. 85-103.

Jeremias, J., *Die Briefe an Timotheus und Titus* Das Neue Testament Deutsch, edited by G. Friedrich, Göttingen: Vandenhoeck und Ruprecht, 1975.

Karris, R. J., 'The Background and Significance of the Polemic of the Pastoral Epistles', *JBL* 92, 1973, pp. 549–564.

Lock, W., *The Pastoral Epistles* ICC, Edinburgh: T. and T. Clark, 1924.

MacMullen, R., 'Women in Public in the Roman Empire', *Historia* 29, 1980, pp. 208–218.

Malherbe, A. J., '"In Season and out of Season", 2 Tim 4.2', *JBL* 103, 1984, pp. 235-243.

— 'Medical Imagery in the Pastorals', *Texts and Testaments*, W. E. March (ed.), San Antonio: Trinity University Press, 1980, pp. 19-35.

Meade, D. G., *Pseudonymity and Canon*. An Investigation of the Relationship of Authorship and Authority in Jewish and Earliest Christian Tradition, Tübingen: J. C. B. Mohr, Paul Siebeck, 1986, Grand Rapids: Eerdmans, 1987.

Meier, J. P., 'Presbyteros in the Pastoral Epistles', *CBQ* 35, 1973, pp. 323–345.

Metzger, B. M., 'A Reconsideration of Certain Arguments against Pauline Authorship of the Pastoral Epistles', *Expository Times* 70, 1958, pp. 91-94.

— 'Literary Forgeries and Canonical Pseudepigrapha', *JBL* 91, 1972, pp. 3-24.

Mott, S. C., 'Greek Ethics and Christian Conversion: the Philonic Background of Titus 2.10-14 and 3.3-7', *Nov T* 20, 1978, pp. 22-48.

Moule, C. F. D., 'The Problem of the Pastoral Epistles, a Reappraisal', *BJRL* 47, 1965, pp. 430-452.

Oden, T. C., *First and Second Timothy and Titus*, Interpretation, Louisville: John Knox Press, 1989.

Pierce, C. W., *Conscience in the New Testament*, Studies in Biblical Theology 15, London: SCM Press, 1955.

Porter, S. E., 'What does it mean to be "saved by childbirth" (1 Tim 2.15)?' *JSNT* 49, 1993, pp. 87–102.

Quinn, J. D., 'The Last Volume of Luke: the Relation of Luke-Acts to the Pastoral Epistles', C. Talbert (ed.) *Perspectives on Luke-Acts*, Edinburgh and Danville: T. and T. Clark, 1978, pp. 62-75.

Skeat, T. C., '"Especially the Parchments": a note on 2 Tim 4.13', *JTS* 30, 1979, pp. 173-177.

Spicq, P. C., *Saint Paul. Les Epîtres Pastorales*, 2 vols. Paris: Gabalda, 4th edition, 1969.

Strobel, A., 'Schreiben des Lukas? Zum sprachlichen Problem der Pastoralbriefe', *NTS* 15, 1969, pp. 191-210.

Thiselton, A. C., 'The Logical Role of the Liar Paradox in Titus 1.12,13. A Dissent from the Commentaries in the Light of Philosophical and Logical Analysis', *Biblical Interpretation* 2, 1994, pp. 207-223.

Towner, P. H. *The Goal of our Instruction. The Structure of Theology and Ethics in the Pastoral Epistles* JSNT SS 34, Sheffield: Sheffield Academic Press, 1989.

Turner, N., Vol 1V of J. H. Moulton *A Grammar of NT Greek*, Edinburgh: T. and T. Clark, 1976, pp. 101-105.

Wilson, S. G., *Luke and the Pastoral Epistles*, London: SPCK, 1979.

Ancient Greek and Latin authors

Critical editions and English translations are available in the Loeb Classical Library, Cambridge, Mass., London: Harvard University Press. Reference will be made to works by the following:

Aristotle, the Greek philosopher, fourth century BCE, whose teachings were recorded by pupils.

Dio Chrysostom, Stoic philosopher, the later first and early second century CE.

Diodorus Siculus, the historian, first century BCE.

Diogenes Laertius, the philosophical writer who recorded the teachings of the various Greek philosophical schools, third century CE.

Epictetus, the Stoic philosopher who lived in the second half of the first century CE and the beginning of the second. His discourses are recorded by his pupil Arrian.

Horace, the Latin poet, first century BCE.

Josephus, the Jewish historian and apologist, second half of the first century CE.

Menander, the comic poet, fourth to third century BCE.

Petronius, the Latin novelist, first century CE.

Philo, the Jewish philosophical apologist from Alexandria, early first century CE.

Plato, the Greek philosopher, fourth century BCE.

Philostratus, the biographer of Apollonius of Tyana, early third century CE.

Plutarch, the historian and moralist, late first and early second century CE.

Polybius, the historian, second century BCE.

Seneca, the Stoic philosopher, who wrote in Latin, early first century CE.

Strabo, the geographer, first century BCE to first century CE.

Xenophon, the historian, fourth century BCE.

Zeno, the founder of Stoic philosophy, fourth to third century BCE.

INTRODUCTION

Like the Epistle to Philemon, those to Timothy and Titus are distinguished from other NT epistles attributed to Paul by their address to individuals rather than to believing communities. In modern New Testaments, these four epistles are found at the end of the Pauline corpus, and they are arranged in order of length, not in an order determined by date or subject matter. But the Pastoral Epistles are also different from Philemon, as their nickname suggests, because they are addressed to individual Pauline delegates with pastoral responsibilities. Timothy and Titus are exhorted to express in word and deed the theological, christological and ethical insights which the epistles contain, in relation to various groups within the believing communities, conceived in I Timothy and Titus as older and younger men and women, and slaves. Those two epistles also give prominence to the generally admired socio-ethical characteristics which local male leaders should possess. In addition, I Timothy pays particular attention to prayers and to the behaviour of male and female believers at community assemblies, to the support of believing widows, and to the appropriate attitudes and actions of rich members. II Timothy encourages believers' faithful endurance of the suffering occasioned by state persecution. All the Pastorals highlight 'healthy teaching' and contrast it with different and diseased teaching. Moreover, they seek to ground their ethical exhortation in beliefs about God and Christ Jesus, and assert that wrong belief issues inevitably in unethical conduct. As in other ancient Hellenistic moral exhortation, they depict examples which help to concretize the more general admonition, and which are offered for emulation or avoidance. Paul becomes the prototypical example for imitation, but occasionally Christ's example is also mentioned. Timothy and Titus are required to accept and to put into practice without question the epistles' instructions, as the commands of an older and wiser apostle. But they are also themselves to become worthy examples, in their teaching, in the manner in which their exhortation and reproof are given, and in their general behaviour. In this way, active participation rather than passive acceptance is demanded.

The Pastorals, however, are not only addressed to two different delegates, but each presupposes a different situation. The epistle to Titus assumes a situation in which a Pauline mission on the island of Crete had met with some initial success, and Titus had been left behind to appoint suitable elders who could refute those contradicting the healthy teaching. At least some of these *insubordinate people* are described as *those of the circumcision* (1.10), so that the genealogies which interest them and the law over which they quarrel, like the Jewish myths, seem to refer to Jewish traditions. Hence, the positive teaching of this epistle echoes some of the emphases found in Romans and Galatians, although without offering full refutations.

The first epistle to Timothy assumes a situation in which Timothy had also been left behind by Paul, but as a Pauline delegate to a more established believing community at Ephesus. Timothy's mission is therefore concerned with reform rather than consolidation. In particular, he is to ensure the proper socio-ethical qualifications of mature male believers who serve as overseer, deacon or elder, and to discipline any wayward elder. The other reason given for leaving him behind is so that he could charge some fellow believers not to offer different teaching, and the epistle encourages him to marginalize and avoid those who are teaching *what is falsely called knowledge* (6.20). There is no suggestion, however, that such people are influenced by Jewish traditions in any negative way. The positive teaching of this epistle promotes an understanding of the believing community as *the household of God* (3.15), focusing on patriarchal responsibilities and the subordination of most young people, all women and all slaves. Similar teaching is found in Titus, but in I Tim it is explicitly grounded theologically.

The second epistle to Timothy assumes a situation in which Paul is now in prison and expecting imminent martyrdom. It represents Paul's last testament. It expects Timothy not only to take a stand against false teaching, an element of which is specified as a belief that the resurrection has happened already, but also repeatedly admonishes him to share in Paul's sufferings. Opponents are those who both betray Paul's teaching and betray him personally. Timothy is exhorted to loyalty through the examples of faithful endurance provided by Christ Jesus and Paul, which are movingly and memorably described. He is also urged to join Paul as Onesiphorus had done. References to suffering pervade the epistle, and all who live *in Christ Jesus* are expected to share them. This setting helps to explain the epistle's tenderness and warmth of expression, but those features also force us to notice the more distant, formal and relatively cold tone of I Timothy and Titus, in spite of their address to close associates. The intimate character of II Timothy is closer to what we might have expected in all correspondence between Paul and Timothy and Titus.

In spite of the diverse situations and addressees, however, the Pastorals are usefully studied together because of their shared pastoral concern, and because of their shared theological, christological and ethical perspectives, expressed in a similar and particular style and vocabulary. For example, they have in common a belief in present salvation, in contrast to other Paulines, as well as a belief in the future eschatological completion of salvation in eternal life. Again, in contrast to other Paulines, they assert that some sayings are sure. Distinctive also is their description of approved teaching as *healthy* or *sound*, and this teaching repeatedly exhorts to *piety* or *godliness* and to *moderation* or *good judgment*. They refer both to Christ's future eschatological *appearing* and to his past *appearing*. I Timothy and Titus also mention the appointment of elders, to whom no reference is made in other Paulines. In their expressions of theology, christology, ethics and community organisation, these epistles are distinctive within the Pauline corpus, and sometimes distinctive within the whole NT.

Some commentaries, like those of Dibelius-Conzelmann and Hanson, are particularly concerned with the identification of sources which may underlie the Pastorals: liturgical confessions and praise, household codes, extracts from writings about church order, traditional Hellenistic ethical teaching, sometimes expressed in brief characterisations of virtuous or vicious people, quotations from and allusions to the Jewish Scriptures, taken over by believing communities. Pursuing these interests tends to give the impression that the Pastorals are mere collections of older material, somewhat arbitrarily arranged. Unfortunately, the form of a commentary, which inevitably has to break up the text into short sections, favours such an impression. But the recent studies by Donelson and Fiore have demonstrated the coherence of these epistles, elucidating the ways in which ethics is anchored theologically and christologically, and in which the explicit and implicit examples serve to fill out the exhortation in more definite portrayals. These character sketches either encourage or discourage conformity, and, by often focusing on historical exemplars, they suggest the real possibility of such forms of living. The commentary will try to demonstrate the coherence, as well as noticing where tensions exist.

Nevertheless, the Pastorals, like all other Christian writings, do take up insights from alternative traditions to enrich their own understandings. Living traditions are constantly in dialogue with rivals, whether explicitly or implicitly. The Pastorals take up the fruits of Jewish Hellenistic reflection, for example, in their short descriptions of the nature of God. They also draw on Hellenistic philosophy, which they mostly integrate into their specifically Christian and Pauline traditions, although, occasionally, opportunities for doing so are missed. For example, I Timothy 6.6-8 expresses Stoic teaching about the contentment afforded by a simple life-style, without attempting to ground that perception through reference to Jesus' life. During the following centuries, Christian writers necessarily drew on Stoicism and Middle- and Neo-Platonism in order to give expression to beliefs in the Trinity and Christ's two natures. In the twentieth century, Christians have been influenced by many alternative traditions: Positivism, Aristotelianism, Idealism, Existentialism, Pragmatism, in order both to express and to develop their beliefs. The Pastorals, then, are part of a great and continuing tradition.

The order in which the epistles appear in the NT will be followed in the commentary, rather than any purported historical order. Each of the epistles is sufficiently self-contained to make sense on its own. Naturally, some cross references among the Pastorals, as well as among the Paulines and the rest of the NT, will sometimes be drawn to readers' attention.

I TIMOTHY

Outline

After an introduction, which presents Paul as a prototypical sinner
who received mercy, so encouraging Timothy to expect that those
who offer different teaching might be changed too, the main body of
the epistle instructs Timothy about various pastoral matters: about
the believing community's prayers and male and female behaviour
at community meetings, about the necessary socio-ethical calibre of
overseer and deacon, about Christ's universal triumph which should
bolster future withstanding of false teachings, about Timothy's
model leadership, and about what or how he is to teach groups
of believers, older and younger men and women, the support
of genuine widows, the treatment of good and bad elders, the
behaviour of slaves and the wealthy. The exhortations evince
common Hellenistic or Jewish Hellenistic concerns but are usually
founded on Christian beliefs.

The opening and introduction to the epistle: contrasting portraits
1.1–20

1.1 As in our culture, Hellenistic letters written in the first and second centuries CE more or less followed conventional patterns, although their conventions differ from ours. The opening, for example, indicates who is writing to whom, sends greetings, and then introduces recipients to the matters which will be addressed in the main section of the work. I Timothy begins with the name of the sender, Paul, and adds a description of his religious standing which justifies his offering advice to others: *apostle of Christ Jesus by command of God our Saviour and Christ Jesus our hope*. The description claims that Paul is someone whom God was commissioning, and the other Pauline writings present apostles as people whose calling gave them both responsibilities and the accompanying authority (e.g. Gal. 1–2; I Cor. 9). An apostle may therefore give instructions to others who are not apostles. The God who is said to command Paul, however, is called *God our Saviour*. This description orientates the reader to expect further references to the salvation which God brings about. Salvation from one form of life and for another form of life will become a major theme of the epistle (see Towner, 1989). But Paul's apostleship and the command are also presented as coming from *Christ Jesus. Christ*, the Greek for anointed one or Messiah, is identified as Jesus. Calling him *our hope* is unique in the NT, although hope is recognised as a Christian disposition (e.g. Rom. 5.4; 8.24) and Col. 1.27 refers to 'this mystery, which is Christ in you, the hope of glory'. *Christ Jesus our hope* directs the reader to his future appearing, a perspective encouraged in this and the other Pastorals (e.g. 6.14; II Tim. 4.1; Titus 2.13). The belief that God saves human beings through Christ Jesus at his first appearing, but that this salvation would only find completion at his future eschatological appearing, frames the rest of the epistle's exhortation (2.3–6; 6.14–16, 19).

1.2   Timothy is identified as the recipient. He is described as *true-born* or *legitimate child in (the) faith*. He is therefore conceived as Paul's subordinate, metaphorically as Paul's child, in need of advice from an older and more experienced 'father'. But calling him Paul's legitimate child implies that he is Paul's true agent, in distinction from others who will be introduced in a moment, people who provide different teaching.

The usual greeting of Hellenistic letters is then given a Christian colouring, as in other NT correspondence. The normal Pauline form, *grace to you and peace*, is expanded to include *mercy*, so introducing an emphasis which will be expanded in 1.12–16. God is then called, metaphorically, *Father*. The metaphor of God as Father, common in the Jewish Scriptures and in other parts of the NT, intimates that both human life itself (6.13) and human well-being (*grace, mercy and peace*) ultimately come from God. The metaphor also implies that human beings should relate to God as 'sons and daughters', and to one another as 'brothers and sisters' in a surrogate family. Unlike other Paulines, however, the Pastorals never explicitly call human beings sons and daughters. Not even Jesus is called son. But the believing community is understood as a *brotherhood* (4.6). The salutation also recognises *Christ Jesus* as *our Lord*, that is, as the Messiah and master to whom devotion and service are due.

1.3–20   recalls why Timothy was left behind at Ephesus, and this sets the scene for further advice in chapters 2–6. While Paul travelled into Macedonia, Timothy was left at Ephesus so that he might *instruct certain people not to teach differently* or, as the REB paraphrases the clause, *to give up teaching erroneous doctrines*. The exact delineation of this different teaching is difficult because mostly general and conventional derogatory epithets are used, like *speculations* and *empty talk*, and the epistle contains no specific refutations (see Karris, 1973). Here, certain people are said to *devote themselves to interminable myths and genealogies which give rise to speculation*, but no particular myths and genealogies are mentioned, either here or in 6.3–5, where the subject is resumed. Commentaries like that of Hanson draw attention to the importance of specific myths and genealogies for second and third century Gnostic writings, but most people in the first and second centuries CE were interested in myths and genealogies of one kind or another (e.g. Polybius 9.2.1; Colson, 1917–18). For example, family genealogies were important in a society in which status and property were inherited from parents.

The people criticised in this passage, however, seem to be members of the believing community. Objection is taken to the endless nature of the myths and genealogies and to the speculation thus encouraged. In other words, whatever these myths and genealogies were, they are characterised as useless, and their unprofitable features are immediately contrasted with *the arrangement or plan of God in the faith*. The orderliness and the comprehensive and complete nature of God's plan suggests that there is no need for speculation. Moreover, the dispositional effects of this plan on believers is highlighted to complete the contrast: *the goal of the instruction is the love which springs from a pure heart and a good conscience and genuine faith*. The reader is encouraged to value these dispositions and to believe in God's plan which engenders them, rather than to be impressed by the pseudo-sophistication of empty speculation. This contrast is reinforced by another reference to those who teach differently, as people who have *gone astray into a wilderness of words*. That their teaching is empty, a common denigration of alternative teaching in Hellenistic literature, is illustrated by suggesting that these teachers wanted to be *teachers of the law* but that they understood neither what they were saying nor the matters about which they were making assertions. The general nature of this characterisation of people who teach differently makes it easy to apply in a variety of particular historical situations, including our own. Unfortunately, even those of us who are gifted in the art of rhetoric sometimes find it hard to distinguish between convincing insights and empty chatter. It is easier to make this distinction in the case of others.

1.5–11 The reference to those who wanted to be teachers of the law allows a digression to explain what the value of the law really is. So *the law* is called *good* (REB *an admirable thing*) as in Rom. 7.16, but the proviso is voiced that *we treat it as law*. The argument is not developed in the manner of Rom. 7, nor is there any concern for Romans' opposition between justification by faith and works of the Scriptural law. Rather, this law is understood to teach *the lawless and unruly* what to avoid. Bad behaviour is characterised in a list which is made memorable in the Greek by assonance and alliteration. *Insubordination* and *impiety* are the opposite of the virtues repeatedly advocated by the Pastorals, *subordination* and *piety* (2.2, 11; 3.4, 16; 4.7–11; 5.4; 6.3, 5–6, 11; II Tim. 3.5, 12; Titus 1.1; 2.5, 9, 12; 3.1). Some of the most heinous human activities, commonly condemned in law codes, are then listed. The ready agreement of the reader that the law is designed to discourage such extreme vice is assumed. No specific reference to the Jewish law, however, is made. Much of the vocabulary is absent from or rare in the Jewish Scriptures. The list epitomises horrendous criminals as those not only condemned by the law but also by *the sound* or *healthy teaching* which the Pastorals promote. There is no suggestion that believers at Ephesus, not even those teaching differently, were guilty of any of these particular deeds. Extreme cases are used for rhetorical effect, to cause repugnance in the reader. They represent the end to which lawlessness tends, in contrast to the *goal of the instruction* which is *love* (verse 5). Finally, the teaching of this digression is said to be in accordance with *the good news* or *gospel of the glory of the ever-blessed God with which I have been entrusted*. The epistle seeks to pass on what had been entrusted to Paul. Both the Dibelius-Conzelmann and Hanson commentaries detect traces of liturgical praise in the final clause.

1.12   The normal Hellenistic epistolary thanksgiving, like the earlier greeting, is given a Christian content in order to expand two matters which had briefly been mentioned earlier: Paul's authority and God's mercy through Christ Jesus. *Christ Jesus* is said to have *empowered* Paul (cf. Phil. 4.13; REB *made him equal to the task*). The reason for this empowerment is then expressed: Christ considered Paul *faithful* or *worthy of trust* (cf. I Cor. 7.25), *appointing me to service*. Fidelity is one of the theological virtues which the Pastorals regard as crucially important (e.g. 3.11; 4.3, 10, 12; 5.16; 6.2; II Tim. 2.2; Titus 1.6; 3.8). Authority is conferred for *service*, not tyranny (cf. I Cor. 16.15).

1.13–16   Moreover, these verses create a portrait of Paul designed to encourage the reader that those who teach differently might also receive mercy. Explicit references to Paul's biography are used in other Paulines as an aid to exhortation, the closest parallel to this passage appearing in the heartfelt expression of I Cor. 15.8–10, where Paul calls himself 'the least of the apostles' and refers to God's grace as affecting his transformation from persecutor to apostle. Here Paul's former life is depicted as that of a *slanderer, persecutor and insulter* of Christ Jesus, and the word *slanderer* is picked up again in the description of those delivered to Satan, mentioned in 1.20 (the REB translation obscures the connexion). Paul is said to have received mercy because he had *acted in the ignorance of unbelief.* No such excuse is offered in other Paulines, and the notion that persecutors and unbelievers act in ignorance is closer to the teaching of Luke–Acts (Luke 23.34; Acts 3.17; 13.27; 17.23, 30). *The grace of our Lord*, probably a reference to the grace of Christ in this context, is said to have been *lavished* on Paul the persecutor, transferring him to the realm of *faith and love* which is *in Christ Jesus*. The common Pauline expression *in Christ* is expanded, as always in the Pastorals, to include the name Jesus (cf. Rom. 6.11, 23; I Cor. 1.2). Moreover, in other Paulines, persons, not dispositions, are usually said to be in Christ. Only Rom. 8.39 is close to this passage. But the Pastorals' major focus on the ethical dispositions which God engenders in Christ Jesus accounts for the change.

Christ's action with regard to Paul is then explained by a general statement about the purpose of Christ's life. It is introduced by a reassuring formula: *here is a saying you may trust*, or, more literally, *the saying is sure*, which is used elsewhere, but only in the Pastorals (3.1; 4.9; II Tim. 2.11; Titus 3.8; cf. a similar formula in Rev 21.5; 22.6). In this instance, a second, conventional affirmation is added: *one that merits acceptance*, as in 4.9, and this has the effect of placing the statement which follows beyond question (cf. Plato, *Timaeus* 49B). Some commentators suggest that the formula always introduces an extract from a commonly held statement of belief about Christ's saving work, and, if this were so, the already accepted statement would form the basis for any further teaching in the section in which the quotation appears. The REB accepts this view and places the statement in inverted commas as a quotation. But the use of the formula in 3.1, where no statement about Christ's saving work appears in the immediate vicinity, makes the suggestion unconvincing. It is more likely that the formula functions to draw the reader's attention to an important insight, whatever the nature of that insight, while encouraging its acceptance. Here the general statement is: *Christ Jesus came into the world to save sinners*. It conceives the whole of Jesus' life as serving this one purpose. *Came into the world* is an expression for *lived a human life* (cf. Wisd 7.6; Leviticus Rabbah 31.6; I Tim. 6.7; Rom. 5.12; I Cor. 15.35). That people are *sinners*, that is, people are alienated from God through their own infidelity and wrong-doing, and that they need to be *saved* from sinning are taken for granted (cf. Matt. 1.21), although this particular expression of the belief has no exact parallel in the NT, the closest being Luke 19.10. The God who is called *Saviour* in 1.1 is now understood to have acted through Jesus, and to have saved people from sinning and thereby destroying their relationship with God. In other words, salvation is conceived, not as something people can achieve through their own efforts, but as something given to them, as an act of *grace* by God through Christ Jesus.

1.16 This central tenet of faith is then illustrated by referring back to the case of Paul, who is now characterised as *the foremost of sinners* (REB *among them I stand first*) who nevertheless *received mercy*. Moreover, his receipt of mercy is construed as an expression of Christ's purpose: so that *Jesus Christ might display his inexhaustible patience*. In this way, Paul becomes *a prototype of those who were to believe in him for eternal life* (the REB paraphrases *I might be typical of all those who were in future to have faith in him and gain eternal life*) . That Paul's case or the case of any other lesser sinner demonstrates Christ's *patience* is without parallel in the rest of the NT. But God's patience with sinners is remarked in the Jewish Scriptures and elsewhere in the NT (e.g. Ps. 86.15; 145.8; Joel 2.13; Rom. 9.22; I Peter 3.20), and here Christ is represented acting as God's agent. Furthermore, Paul, the foremost of sinners, is seen as a prototype for all lesser sinners whom Christ would save, including those just criticised for offering different teaching. It is this belief in Christ Jesus, and the assertions about the change which such belief engenders, which is said finally to bring *eternal life*. In Dan. 12.2, the only place where eternal life is mentioned in the Jewish Scriptures, it refers to post-mortem eternal life, given by God at the eschaton, and that is the meaning here (cf. Rom. 5.21; Gal. 6.8; Titus 1.2; 3.7).

The passage therefore ends appropriately with praise of the God who had brought all this about through Christ Jesus. That God is *imperishable* or *immortal* is often asserted in Hellenistic philosophy, and was taken over by Jewish Hellenistic writers (e.g. Diog. L. 10.123; Philo, *Moses* 2.171; Josephus, *Ant.* 10.278), and by Paul in Rom. 1.23, the only NT parallel. Similarly, that God is *invisible* was also taken over from Hellenistic philosophy by Philo (*Moses* 2.65), Josephus (*War* 7.346) and Paul (Rom. 1.20; cf. Col. 1.15; Heb. 11.27; cf. also Deut. 4.15). Here we see the enrichment of Jewish reflection by Greek. That this God is *the only God* is asserted in the Jewish Scriptures (e.g. II Kings 19.15, 19; Isa. 37.20) and the NT (Jude 25; cf. John 5.44; Rom. 16.27; I Tim. 6.15). *Eternal King* is literally *King of Ages*, that is, King of this age and the coming age, and to him is attributed *honour and glory for ever and ever*, echoing Jewish liturgical expressions (Tob. 13.6, 10; LXX Ps. 83.4; cf. Gal. 1.5; Phil. 4.20). The Hebrew *amen* is taken over from the Jewish Scriptures as an affirmation (e.g. I Chron. 16.36; Neh. 5.13; 8.6; Tob. 8.8; cf. Rom. 1.25; 9.5).

1.18–20 The final three verses of the chapter return to the topic of Timothy's task in relation to those who were teaching differently (see 1.3–7). The REB's *by those prophetic utterances which first directed me to you* is a possible but not a necessary translation of the Greek (cf. 4.14), which could also mean *in accordance with preceding prophecies for you* and which might refer to the Spirit's prediction of apostasies, as in 4.1. Either interpretation would justify Timothy's resistance to contrary teaching. The metaphor of fighting is also found in II Cor. 10.3–6. Timothy is to fight, not by the use of violence, but by offering healthy teaching and by exemplifying the ethical life it engenders. For his task, he is encouraged to hold *faith* and *a good conscience* (see 1.5; 3.9). By contrast, some are said, *by spurning conscience*, to have *made shipwreck with regard to the faith* (REB's *of their faith* does not capture the sense of the Greek). Here *the faith* refers to the Christian faith as defined by the epistle. *Conscience* is the capacity to react against religious and ethical wrongs. The people criticised are not in such a parlous state as those with corrupted consciences, mentioned in Titus 1.15, since they are described as rejecting a conscience which was not yet completely insensitive. Two of the people are named: Hymenaeus and Alexander, counter-examples to Paul and Timothy, and Paul is said to have *consigned them to Satan, that they might learn not to slander* (REB *be blasphemous* obscures the connexion between Paul as a former slanderer and these two slanderers). In I Cor. 5.5, Paul advocates that a man who was living with his stepmother should be delivered to Satan. Exclusion from the believing community is understood as delivery into Satan's realm, but the action is conceived as salutary, and the Pauline biographical references above encourage the expectation that these men too would be saved by God's grace and mercy in Christ Jesus.

This introductory chapter has created three portraits: that of Paul, the foremost of sinners who received mercy, and who became an apostle by God's command; that of Timothy, his legitimate child and representative, who should fight opponents with faith and a good conscience; and that of false teachers fond of myths, genealogies and speculations, who desired to be teachers, of the law but lacked understanding, who had rejected conscience, and two of whom Paul had already turned over to Satan to bring about a change in their lives like the change God through Christ Jesus had brought to his life. In this way, the scene has been set for further instruction and exhortation in the main body of the letter, from 2.1 to 6.19, after which a final general admonition leads into the grace (6.20–21).

Notes on 1.1–20

1.1 *By command of God* Usually, the Paulines refer to the *will of God*, cf. I Cor. 1.1; II Cor. 1.1; Eph. 1.1; Col. 1.1; II Tim. 1.1.

Christ Jesus In other Paulines, the designation *Christ Jesus* occurs alongside the equally frequent *Jesus Christ*. In the Pastorals, however, *Christ Jesus* is more common, with *Jesus Christ* only in 1.16; 6.3, 14; II Tim. 2.8; Titus 3.6.

1.2 *Timothy* Elsewhere in the Paulines, he is called Paul's fellow worker (Rom. 16.21), brother, in a metaphorical sense (II Cor. 1.1; Philemon 1), a fellow slave of Christ (Phil. 1.1), and Paul's beloved and faithful child (I Cor. 4.17), whom he sent on missions (I Cor. 4.17; 16.10; Phil. 2.19; I Thess. 3.2, 6; see also Acts 16.1; 17.14–15; 18.5; 19.22; 20.4; Heb. 13.23).

Mercy God's mercy through Christ Jesus is a special concern of the Pastorals: 1.12–16; II Tim. 1.2, 16, 18; Titus 3.5; cf. Gal. 6.16.

Christ Jesus our Lord Jesus, the anointed one or Messiah, is recognised as our Lord. Only in II Tim. 4.1, 18, however, is any mention made of his eschatological or heavenly kingdom. I Tim. will highlight his present universal triumph (3.16). Calling Jesus Lord does not imply that he is God, but recognises his human kingly status. Those who ruled kingdoms were habitually called lord (cf. I Sam. 22.12; II Sam. 14.9, 12, 15; 19.20; Ps. 110.1). Distinguishing Jesus as *our Lord* acknowledges the specifically Christian commitment to him.

1.3 *Not to teach differently* The verb is found only here and at 6.3 in the NT.

Macedonia and *Ephesus* The geographical reference cannot be fitted into Acts' account of Paul's and Timothy's journeys, but may be understood as following on from the travel plans of I Cor. 16.5–11.

1.4 *Myths* cf. Philo, *Abraham* 76.

Speculation The word is found nowhere else in surviving ancient Greek literature.

God's arrangement or plan cf. 'the plan of the mystery' in Eph. 3.9. Clement of Alexandria uses the word in the sense of training, *Paed.* 1.18.69, 3. Note that the root of the Greek word is connected with household arrangements, and leads naturally into the image of the church as the household of God in 3.15.

1.5 *Pure heart* Emphasis on the need for a heart devoted to God is typical of the Jewish Scriptures (e.g. Ezek. 36.26). Compare Rom. 5.5 'the love of God poured into our hearts'. Only here and in II Tim. 2.2 among the Paulines is heart defined by *pure* cf. Ps. 24.4; Matt. 5.5, but I Thess. 3.13 expresses a similar meaning with *hearts unblamable in holiness*.

Good conscience In the Pastorals, conscience is never used without further definition, as it is in Romans and I and II Corinthians. The kind of conscience approved in the Pastorals is either good, as here, or pure (1.19; 3.9; II Tim. 1.3). This good or pure conscience allows people to react against religious and ethical wrongdoing (cf. Philo, *Special Laws* 1.203, and the study by C. A. Pierce, 1955).

Sincere faith Rom. 12.9 and II Cor. 8.6 encourage sincere love, but only here and II Tim. 1.5 in the NT is faith defined as sincere. The adjective serves to differentiate this kind of faith from a faith which is used for gain, 6.3–5.

1.6 *Gone astray* or literally *missed the mark* cf. 6.21 *missed the mark as regards the faith* and II Tim. 2.18 *missed the mark as regards the truth* . The expression is confined to the Pastorals in the NT, cf. Plutarch *On listening to lectures* 15, and *Tabletalk VII* 3, *Mor.* 46A, 705C.

Turn away or *run after* cf. 5.15; 6.20; II Tim. 4.4; Epictetus 1.6.42; Philo, *Special Laws* 2.23. In the NT, the expression is found only in the Pastorals and in Heb. 12.13.

A wilderness of words or literally *idle talk* In the NT, the expression occurs only here, with the related adjective in Titus 1.10 cf. Plutarch, *On educating children* 9, *Mor.* 6F.

1.7 *Teachers of the law* The word is used elsewhere in the NT only in Luke 5.17; Acts 5.34, where the contexts show that it refers to Jewish teachers of the Jewish law. Here, however, the law is neither described as Jewish nor do 1.9–10 echo summaries of the Jewish law like the Decalogue (contra Kelly, see below on 1.9–10).

1.8 *As law* or literally *lawfully* In the NT, the word is found only here and II Tim. 2.5, cf. IV Macc. 6.18; Josephus, *Against Apion* 2.152, 217.

1.9–10 Lists of vices or vicious people were used as a common teaching device in Hellenistic philosophical literature, and were taken up in Jewish Hellenistic writings, as in Christian, cf. Philo, *Abel and Cain* 32. In this list, the following words are found nowhere else in the NT: *parricides, matricides, murderers, kidnappers, perjurers*. Moreover, *unholy* (REB) is found only in the Pastorals. None of these words is found in the Torah of the LXX either, and *murderers* only in IV Macc. 9.28; *kidnappers* only in III Macc. 7.5; *perjurers* only in Zech 5.3; and *unholy* only in Esth. 8.13 and III Macc. 1.21. *Liars* (cf. Titus 1.10) represents the opposite of those *who come to a knowledge of the truth* (2.4), expressed in the healthy teaching (1.10).

1.10 *Sound/healthy teaching* Medical metaphors are used in the

Pastorals, as in Hellenistic philosophical literature, but not in the other Paulines, to characterise both good and bad teaching. So, good teaching is again called healthy in 6.3; II Tim1.13; 4.3; Titus 1.9, 13; 2.1, cf. also Titus 2.2, 8, while in II Tim. 2.17 bad teaching is said to eat its way like gangrene. See A. J. Malherbe, 1980.

1.11 *Glory* cf. II Cor. 4.4, 6; Col. 1.27.

Blessed God is a Hellenistic expression which was taken over by Hellenistic Judaism, cf. Diog. L. 10.123; Philo, *Special Laws* 2.53; Josephus, *Ant.* 10.278; *Against Apion* 2.190. It does not mean that people bless God, but that God's life expresses every blessing and that God gives blessings to people. Contrast the terminology in Rom. 1.25; 9.5.

1.12 *I give thanks* Here and II Tim. 1.3, the Greek expression conforms to that of non-Christian Hellenistic letters, whereas Pauline phraseology in other epistles is different e.g. Rom. 1.8; I Cor. 1.4.

1.13 *Insulter* (REB *with outrage*) is used in the NT only here and in the list of vicious people in Rom. 1.30.

1.14 *Lavished* is used only here in the NT.

Faith and love in combination, cf. Philemon 5; Eph. 1.15; 3.17; 6.23; II Tim. 1.13.

1.15 *Here is a saying you can trust* See the article by Campbell, 1994, which discusses possible interpretations, but tries to retain the suggestion that it introduces a quotation about Christ's saving work by identifying the saying to which I Tim. 3.1 refers as that in 3.16. Had the introduction referred to that saying, however, there is no convincing reason why it should not have appeared in 3.16.

1.16 *Prototype* In the NT only here and in II Tim. 1.13, but the word is common in Hellenistic writings, e.g. Diog. L. 9.78; Philo, *Abraham* 71.

1.19 *Shipwreck* as a metaphor for moral or religious disaster, cf. Philo, *Change of Names* 215.

1.20 *Hymenaeus* is mentioned only here and II Tim. 2.17, where he is represented as someone whose talk eats its way like gangrene because he and Philetus had swerved from the truth by holding that the resurrection has happened already.

Alexander An Alexander is also mentioned in II Tim. 4.14, where he is called a coppersmith and is said to have done Paul great but unspecified harm. It is unlikely that he should be identified with the Alexanders of Mark 15.21; Acts 4.6 or 19.33, since Alexander was a common name.

Prayer
2.1–7

Placed *first* in the new instructions to Timothy, prayer is presented as the necessary prerequisite for improving the life of the believing community. Through Timothy, the whole community is encouraged to offer prayers to God, not only *petitions* and *intercessions* but also *thanksgivings*, like those already voiced in 1.12. And these prayers are to be offered *for everyone*, not merely for members of the believing community. It is assumed that God's purpose encompasses all people, and that believers should share that concern. The special mention of *sovereigns and all in high office*, however, is immediately related to the believing community's welfare. These non-Christian authorities could determine whether believers would live *a tranquil and quiet life in piety and dignity* (REB renders *piety* as *religion*). Here, *piety* and *dignity* or *reverence* seem to suggest dispositions towards rulers as well as towards God. These rulers were powerful in that social world which the epistle understands to be God's world (cf. Rom. 13.1), and, at the very least, they might prevent civic unrest and riot. Since believers did not participate in Graeco-Roman worship, however, they could be suspected of disloyalty, especially if they came to the notice of governors through bad relations with their non-believing neighbours. The epistle will insist that believing leaders should enjoy the respect of outsiders (3.7, 13), and that believing slaves of pagan masters should be models of good service (6.1). There is no unambiguous suggestion in I Tim. that believers were suffering active state persecution, as there is in II Tim, but this kind of teaching may have been given to prevent persecution.

Some commentators (e.g. Dibelius-Conzelmann, Houlden, Hanson) construe this teaching as the expression of bourgeois concerns, concerns to find a secure life in a continuing world, once the hope of an imminent parousia had faded. Kidd's study (1990), however, has shown not only that modern categories like 'bourgeois' are inappropriately applied to first and second century society, but also that the teaching concerning the rich actually undermines their conventional expectations through an appeal for devotion to the God who will grant eternal life at the eschaton (6.17–19). Similarly, MacDonald's study (1988) shows how important is the belief in an eschatological transformation for making sense of the Pastorals' ethical teaching. The hope of Jesus' future appearing (1.1 and 6.14) frames the rest of I Tim.'s teaching. Nevertheless, it is true that the Pastorals contain no profound criticism of the wisdom of this world, as does I Cor. 1–2, and no sense that the whole of creation is subjected to futility and longs for the revealing of the sons of God, as does Romans 8 (see Horrell, 1993). Moreover, only in II Tim. do we find an emphasis on believers' necessary endurance of suffering in this world, in a manner comparable to Philippians, Romans 12, and II Cor. 11–12. There is a difference, however, between enduring persecutions when they come, as II Tim. encourages people to do, and inviting persecutions, which I Tim. discourages.

2.4   The exhortation that prayers should be offered *for everyone* or *for all people* is grounded theologically and christologically. God is again called Saviour, but now the description is explained: *who desires all people to be saved and to come to a knowledge of the truth* (REB paraphrases *whose will it is that all should find salvation and come to know the truth*). The earlier reference to Paul's life (1.12–17) had made it clear that people would be saved from ignorance and from sinning, and would be saved through Christ Jesus' mercy and empowerment. Now emphasis is placed on God's purpose to save all human beings, and the Christian faith is conceived as *knowledge of the truth*, that is, the truth of God's purpose for humanity (cf. II Tim. 2.25; 3.7; Titus 1.1; and, in relation to Judaism, Philo, *Special Laws* 4.178). And it is a truth to be lived, not just apprehended, although it is appealed to rather than argued for, as it would have been by classical Greek philosophers like Plato. This clear emphasis on God's purpose to save all people is one of the Pastorals' major contributions to NT theology.

2.5–6a   The succinct and balanced form of these verses suggests to many commentators that it is a quotation from a Christian creed or liturgy, but, since the actual statements are precisely those required to ground the argument, it is not impossible that they were written for the first time in this epistle, in a memorable form, for just this purpose. If there is *one God*, conceived as both Creator and Saviour, then it follows that God's purpose is to save *all people*. Jesus' role in God's salvation plan is then explained. He is understood as a *human being* (REB *man*) who is *mediator* or *arbitrator* between two parties, God and all human beings. We should notice the universality of the conception: Jesus is conceived as the mediator between God and all people, not between God and the covenant community (see 3.16). The epistle's sophisticated expression of God's transcendence (1.17) highlights the gulf between God and mortal human sinners. Hence, Jesus is presented as the human *mediator* between this God and all human beings. The Jewish philosophical apologist Philo shares with I Tim. this appreciation of God's transcendence, and presents Moses as the human mediator (*Moses* 2.166).

2.6   Moreover, Jesus' whole existence is conceived as a *self-giving ransom* for all people (REB paraphrases *who sacrificed himself to win freedom for all mankind*). Taking up the language of ransoming slaves and captives, Jesus, by giving himself, is understood potentially to ransom all others from the captivity which sinning expresses (see 1.15). The image is not developed, as it was in later Christian theology, to answer the question to whom the price was paid. Rather, this passage emphasises the universal significance of Jesus' self-giving. The significance is then spelt out. Jesus' self-giving life is *the witness at its own time* (REB paraphrases *revealing God's purpose at God's good time*), the witness to the truth about God's purpose (2.4). The reference to *its own time* serves to exclude any suggestion that, since Jesus lived late in human history, he could not have played a central role in God's eternal purpose. Since Jesus lived when he did, and since he is conceived as the mediator between God and all people, God's eternal purpose must have become manifest in his life at the proper time.

2.7   This understanding of Jesus' significance in God's plan to save everyone then explains Paul's appointment as *herald, apostle and teacher of Gentiles* (REB *to instruct the Gentiles*). Paul, the reader had already been told, has been sent by God and Christ Jesus (1.1), but now it is made clear that he has been sent to declare and explain God's purpose to Gentiles in the Graeco-Roman world. It is in furtherance of this mission that the epistle is addressed to his delegate at Ephesus. The asseveration, *this is no lie, it is the truth*, stresses the importance of Paul's mission and the authority it implies. *In faith and truth* (REB *in the true faith* does not capture the sense of the

15

Greek) refers to Paul's fidelity in carrying out the task for which he was appointed.

Notes on 2.1–7

2.1 *Intercessions* is found only here and 4.5 in the NT, but is common in Hellenistic papyri concerned with secular intercessions. I Tim. brings it into the religious sphere.

2.2 *Prayers for sovereigns and all in high office* were a common feature of Jewish Hellenistic literature and are here taken into the Christian tradition; cf. II Macc. 3.11; Josephus, *Ant.* 9.3.

Dignity/reverence is advocated in the NT only by the Pastorals (see also 3.4; Titus 2.7) but the virtue was prized by Hellenistic philosophers (e.g. Epictetus 1.16.13) and Hellenistic Jewish writers (e.g. Josephus, *Life* 258). The Hellenistic household codes, which have exerted an influence on 3.1–13 and 6.1–2, seem to have been influential here too, cf. Titus 3.1; I Peter 2.11–3.7; Epictetus 2.17.3; and see Verner, 1983.

2.4 *Knowledge of the truth* cf. II Tim. 2.25; 3.7; Titus 1.1, with reference to the Christian faith; Epictetus 2.20.21, with reference to Stoic philosophical reflection; Philo, *Every Good Man is Free* 74, with reference to Judaism.

2.5 *One mediator between God and human beings* cf. Job 9.32–33. This Hellenistic legal language is also applied to Moses as the mediator of the covenant (e.g. Philo, *Moses* 2.166). In the NT, the term describes Christ's role only here and in Heb. 8.6; 9.15; 12.24, where Christ is understood as the mediator of the new covenant. The Pastorals' universalism is distinctive.

2.6 *Ransom* The word is used only here in the NT, but a shorter form of the same word is used in Matt. 20.28; Mark 10.45. The shorter form of the related verb is found in Titus 2.14.

Its own time cf. 6.15; Titus 1.3; Gal. 4.4.

2.7 *Herald* cf. II Tim1.11; II Peter 2.5; Epictetus 3.22.69. Other Paulines use the related abstract noun for 'preaching' e.g. Rom. 16.25; I Cor. 1.21.

Teacher of the Gentiles cf. Gal. 1.16; 2.2; Eph. 3.6.

Advice about appropriate behaviour for men and women at community assemblies
2.8–15

2.8–12 The previous paragraph had exhorted Timothy to encourage believers in praying for all people. Now instructions are given which concern the kinds of behaviour considered appropriate to believers when the community met together, distinguishing that relating to men from that relating to women. *Anger or argument* (cf. Phil. 2.14; Col. 3.8), to be avoided, is assumed to be a male rather than a female vice. According to 6.3–5, those who offer different teaching exhibit this vice. *Everywhere* seems to imply that the number of believers at Ephesus required more than one assembly of believers. Female failings are assumed to express themselves in showy dress (cf. I Peter 3.1–5). Very few women in the first and second centuries, however, would have been wealthy enough to appear in such splendour, with *gold or pearls,* but an exaggerated picture has a stronger rhetorical effect. Instead, what is recommended for *women who profess reverence for God* (REB *who claim to be religious)* is *orderly deportment* (REB *dress in a becoming manner), with modesty and chastity* (REB *modestly and soberly). Orderly deportment* carries a moral connotation which would show itself in simple dress. The word translated *chastity,* which appears in the NT only here and in 2.15, when used of men, means 'moderation or good judgment' and was considered a cardinal virtue by Greeks (e.g. Aristotle, *Rhet.* 1.9.9), but, when applied to women, it was often linked with *modesty,* and came to mean *chastity,* that is, moderation in sexual relations (e.g. Xenophon, *Cyrus* 8.1.30–31; Philo, *Special Laws* 1.103; 3.51). Here, such dispositions are said to generate *good deeds.* Female good works, however, are not understood to encompass all the good works which men might perform. Both men and women are warned against insubordination (1.9), but only women are excluded from a public teaching role in the church – *I do not permit women to teach* – and are expected to *listen quietly*. They are not to *have authority over/ dictate to a man /husband*. Had they simply been discouraged from domineering behaviour, advice about them would have matched advice about men elsewhere in the epistle (e.g. 5.1–2; 6.11, 17–18), but this refusal of a public teaching role for women contradicts other Pauline teaching (I Cor. 11.5; Phil. 4.2–3; and the references to women as Paul's fellow workers in Rom. 16).

2.13–14   The refusal is bolstered by an interpretation of Genesis 2–3. According to Gen 2.7, Adam was formed first and then Eve (cf. I Cor. 11.8 but contrast 11.12). The argument takes for granted that priority in time endows superior authority, but such an assumption is not made in the case of Jesus (2.6). The language of deception comes from Gen 3.13, but the declaration that Adam was not deceived and that *it was the woman who, yielding to deception, fell into sin*, although it agrees with the letter, hardly agrees with the spirit of the Genesis passage, according to which both Adam and Eve were held responsible and punished (Gen 3.14–24; but cf. Ecclus 25.24 and contrast Rom. 5.12–21; I Cor. 15.21–22). Many interpreters of the Pastorals, like, most recently, Verner (1983) and MacDonald (1988), suggest that this emphasis on the deception of Eve arises from fears that women were being deceived into following false teachers (5.15; II Tim. 3.6–7), but the Pastorals never depict the false teachers themselves as women, and there is a simpler explanation of this refusal to allow women to teach (see below).

2.15   The form of Eve's punishment, according to Gen 3.16 (the multiplication of pain in childbirth yet her desire for her husband), seems to lie behind the reference to child-bearing. The expression *saved through child-bearing* (REB paraphrases *but salvation for the woman will be in the bearing of children)*, however, is both ambiguous and puzzling. In the Pastorals, *save* usually refers to God's saving people through Christ Jesus from ignorance and sinning (1.15; 2.3–4; 4.16). If *through* is understood to mean *during*, the statement would offer assurance to believing women that they would be saved from pain and possible death during child-bearing. This interpretation would fit with the epistle's interest in the present effects of salvation, and would discourage women who were afraid of child-bearing from adopting celibacy (4.3; 5.11–15). Unfortunately, however, the assurance, so understood, makes no mention of the many kinds of biological malfunction which cause pain and death to women in childbirth, and which first and second century medicine was powerless to alleviate. If this is the correct interpretation, startling miracles would be involved, but healing miracles are mentioned nowhere else in the Pastorals. Moreover, Porter (1993) has cogently argued that *through* must be understood in an instrumental sense, and this interpretation raises other problems. It would contradict all the other teaching about salvation contained in this epistle, and it would exclude infertile and unmarried women from salvation. Only in the final clause of this passage are virtues advocated which other parts of I Tim. see as expressions of a saved life: *faith and love and holiness with chastity*. Whichever interpretation is preferred, the argument hardly bears scrutiny. These reasons for refusing a teaching role to women while allowing it to men are unconvincing.

The misogyny which this passage shares with Ecclesiasticus expresses commonly held, male, conservative Hellenistic attitudes to women. Although Roman women among the elite had achieved some financial independence, and might act as sponsors of associations and engage in business activities (see MacMullen 1980), Greek philosophical literature continued to emphasise the matronly virtues as an ideal for women, as I Tim. does. And the reason for this is not difficult to discern. The Roman Empire, and the Hellenistic empires which preceded it, were gained and retained by military force. The ideal man was conceived as courageous in war and effective in diplomacy. In such a society, men considered it essential that women should give birth to children, especially to male children who could defend the empire in the next generation. But Christian communities understood God's purpose for human beings to be different. Jesus, confessed as the Messiah, had been neither a warrior nor a diplomat, but, on the contrary, had suffered a cruel death at the hands of his enemies without offering violent resistance. The kingdom to which Christians looked forward would not be brought about by human military efforts. Nowhere in the NT is the kind of courage required by warriors advocated. Rather, as in II Tim., believers are urged to endure persecution without retaliation. This new understanding of God's purpose could engender a new social ethos in which women could participate as fully as men, and which other Paulines not only envision (Gal. 3.28) but also encourage in practice (Rom. 16; I Cor. 7 and 11; Phil. 4.2–3). But this new ethos could appear threatening to men, both outside and within believing communities. And believing men could attempt to justify old attitudes and practices by appeal to

19

those parts of the Jewish Scriptures which share them, as I Tim. tries to do in this section. This has led to male insistence that women should be subordinated to men and brought under the control of husbands (2.11–15; 5.14). Husbands, not God or Christ, are to be women's masters. The epistle fails to accord to believing women the kind of responsible agency it accords to believing men, so limiting what elsewhere it asserts about the effects of God's and Christ's grace and mercy. In this way, it deprives the churches of women's valuable service in teaching as well as in other public roles.

It is easy for us, twenty centuries later, to recognise the way in which cultural assumptions have prevented men from noticing the potential of half the human race, women, and have led to a restricted understanding of the power of God's grace in this part of the epistle. It is far more difficult for us to become aware of our own cultural assumptions, which have deadened our appreciation of other human beings, and which underpin a society in which sexism, racism and classism still engender injustice. But the epistle's insights, which have led to its presentation of Jesus as the mediator between God and the whole of humanity, its insistence that believers pray for all people, and its affirmation that God's grace transforms people's lives, can still encourage believers to express their beliefs in practices which do not belie them.

Notes on 2.8–15

2.10 *Reverence for God* The noun is found only here in the NT, but the adjective appears in John 9.31, cf. Gen. 20.11; Job 28.28.
Orderly deportment The expression is used only here in the NT and seems to be adopted from Hellenistic philosophical literature, e.g. Epictetus 2.10.15.
Good deeds are often encouraged in the Pastorals, e.g. 5.10, 25; 6.18. The expression is absent from most of the Paulines, but compare Eph. 2.10; Heb. 10.24.
2.11 *With due submission/ with all submissiveness* cf. Eph. 5.21–22; Col. 3.18; Titus 2.5; I Peter 3.1, 5. I Cor. 14.34–35, which appears in different places in surviving manuscripts, seems originally to have been a marginal gloss expressing views similar to those of I Tim. It contradicts the acceptance of women as prophets who spoke publicly in church assemblies (I Cor. 11 and 14), and it assumes all women would have husbands whom they could question at home, which contradicts the advice to women about remaining unmarried in I Cor. 7.

2.12 *Dictate to/ have authority over* The expression is found only here in the NT but occurs in surviving first century BCE papyri from Egypt.

2.15 *Saved through child-bearing* The attempt to remove the difficulties of interpretation by supposing that the expression refers to the birth of Christ, most recently by Knight (1992), is unconvincing. Had Christ's birth been the subject, the name, Christ Jesus, would have been highlighted, as in 1.15 and 2.5.

The socio-ethical character required for those men who serve the community as leaders

3.1–16

Overseer (REB bishop)

3.1–7

After a general consideration of believers' conduct at community assemblies, the epistle turns to the particular subject of community leadership. *Here is a saying you can trust* introduces and confirms the following statement: *if anyone aspires to the office of overseer, he desires a good work* (REB paraphrases *to aspire to leadership is an honourable ambition*). Serving in the office of an overseer is endorsed as one among many good works recommended by the epistle. This assurance corresponds to that made about the diaconate in 3.13. I Tim. assumes that various groups of male leaders, elders, overseer(s) and deacons, already helped the community at Ephesus, and their responsibilities are largely taken for granted, not described. This makes it difficult to determine what their particular tasks are meant to be, and how one group of leaders relates to another. In the light of second- and third-century practice, some commentators (e.g. H. von Campenhausen, 1969, pp. 106–123) notice the singular *overseer* in I Tim. 3.2 and Titus 1.7, in contrast to the plural in Phil. 1.1; Acts 20.28, and suggest that the local church envisaged by the Pastorals was ruled over by a single monarchical bishop (overseer), who exercised authority over the council of elders (4.14), over the deacons, and over the whole community. But in Titus 1.5–9, *overseer* describes the role which all elders would perform, the singular being generic. The function of elders in Titus, however, is, in one respect, different from the function given them in I Tim. 5.17, since, according to Titus 1.9, all elders are required to teach, while, apparently, only some elders are preachers and teachers, according to I Tim. 5.17. This suggests that the function of elders might differ from community to community, and depend on the particular church's needs. According to I Tim. 3.2, the overseer should be an effective teacher. In I Tim., therefore, the following relationship between elder and overseer seems to be presupposed: elders who taught were called overseers (see J. P. Meier, 1973). This interpretation takes the singular *overseer* as generic, as it is in Titus. An alternative suggestion (e.g. by Dibelius-Conzelmann), that the council of elders was ruled by a single elder who was called overseer, is less convincing because I Tim. 5.17 envisages more than one elder engaged in teaching, a duty which 3.2 gives to the overseer.

3.2–5   The only other duty required of the overseer is that he should be *hospitable* (also Titus 1.8), but that virtue is also required of some widows in 5.10, and was a commonly admired quality. It should not be understood to imply that leaders needed to be rich (contra Verner), since hospitality involves sharing whatever is available, irrespective of whether it is little or much. The other qualifications for overseer, as for deacons, are socio-ethical and correspond to Hellenistic conceptions of the ideal leader, whatever his particular leadership role. The Dibelius-Conzelmann commentary provides parallel Hellenistic examples in appendices, to which may be added Plutarch, *Precepts of Statecraft* 31, *Mor*. 822F–823B (contrast the conception of charismatic leadership, irrespective of marital status and gender, in I Cor. 12.4–11, 27–31). It is not surprising, therefore, that some of these qualities are encouraged more generally in other contexts: *sober and temperate* or *moderate* for all older men in Titus 2.2; *forbearing and avoiding quarrels*   for all believers in Titus 3.2. *Husband of one wife*, a requirement for both overseer and deacon, however, is difficult to interpret. It could exclude polygamy, but, by the first century CE, the practice was uncommon. It could exclude men who had divorced and remarried (forbidden for all believing couples in I Cor. 7.11, 15–16). It could exclude remarried widowers, but, if so, this would be another example of different behaviour encouraged for men and women (5.14). What is clear is that this qualification excludes unmarried men, and all women and slaves, from the office of overseer. At this stage in the epistle, it is unsurprising to find that women are excluded, but the exclusion of unmarried men is striking because elsewhere (I Cor. 7.7) Paul declares that he is unmarried and encourages others with a charismatic gift to remain unmarried. But the Pastorals' restriction of leadership to married men, and, moreover, to a married man who could *manage his houshold well, keeping his children submissive and respectful in every way* (REB paraphrases *controls his children without losing his dignity),* reflects a common assumption about the correct ordering of society in the Graeco-Roman world. It was assumed that free men had the responsibility of keeping in order and submission their wives and children (whatever their ages), as well as any servants and slaves, if they were rich enough to engage or own them. Elite rich men also fulfilled the roles of sponsoring associations, and acted as benefactors of cities, as well as providing support for other free men in need, who might be friends or clients. And the people who were benefitted or ruled over owed loyalty and honour to their patrons. In other words, it was a paternalistic society. In I Tim. 6.17–19, the teaching about the wealthy undermines these social expectations, but in I Tim. 3, the expectation that a well-ordered group would be ruled by free, married, family men is endorsed. The assumption is not unknown in modern Western society.

Moreover, I Tim. 3.5 gives a reason for this advice: *for if a man does not know how to manage his own household, how can he care for God's church?* (REB paraphrases *how can he take charge of a congregation of God's people).* This reasoning would have seemed self-evidently convincing to first and second century men. It implies that the church is like a household in which father figures act as leaders and keep ordinary members in submission. The perception is grounded theologically in 3.15 by calling the church God's household; (cf. I Peter 4.17). A more common NT understanding of the Christian community is also found in I Tim., that of a surrogate family of brothers and sisters under God's fatherhood (1.2; 4.6; 5.1–2; 6.2; cf. II Tim. 1.2; 4.21). But the Pastorals lack the conception of the church as the body of Christ, explored in Rom. 12 and I Cor. 12, a conception which both promotes community over individual and encourages an egalitarian ethos of service. Of course, the image of the church as God's household could also have issued in a more egalitarian community ethos, had God been understood as the only father with community members relating as brothers and sisters. But, in the Pastorals, it serves to endorse the power and responsibility of male patriarchs.

We should notice, however, that, in relation to the household both of the overseer and of the deacon, no mention is made of slaves, who are considered in a separate section (6.1–2, cf. Titus 2.9–10). Verner's study (1983), and even, to a lesser extent, Kidd's (1990), assume too readily that any mention of household would include slaves, but slaves were expensive both to buy and to support, and would not have formed part of most households. The absence of any mention of slaves in I Tim. 3 and Titus 1.5–9, as well as the reference to financial support for elders in I Tim. 5.17, suggest that wealth was not a qualification for leadership (contra Verner), and this, together with the teaching about the rich in 6.17–19, distinguishes the Pastorals' ideal leadership from that of the larger society.

3.6–7 To return to the details of I Tim. 3.1–7, another qualification for the office of overseer is mentioned and justified: he is not to be *newly planted*, a metaphor for a *recent convert*. This requirement could not be made in Titus 1.5–9 because that epistle depicts all believers as new converts. The reason for the exclusion is: *he may be puffed up with conceit and fall into the condemnation of the slanderer* (REB paraphrases *conceit might bring on him the devil's punishment*). *Slanderer* could refer either to the devil or to a human slanderer. If it is taken to refer to the devil, it is unclear what *the condemnation of the devil* means. Would the new convert incur the same condemnation by God as the devil receives, or would he receive a condemnation which the devil has contrived for him? Finally, the instruction requires that the overseer should be well thought of by outsiders, and, again, this is justified: *so that he may not fall into disgrace and the snare of the slanderer*, either human or the devil (cf. II Tim. 2.26. The REB paraphrases *he may not be exposed to scandal and be caught in the devil's snare*). Since the socioethical qualities demanded were generally admired in Graeco-Roman society, a good reputation should be assured, and this could save the community from contempt and even from persecution. The list of characteristics creates a portrait of a moderate man in control of his passions. Spontaneity and enthusiam were not valued in educated Hellenistic circles as they are by some people today. Moreover, the way in which this teaching is justified theologically depends on an interpretation of the concept of the church as God's household. It is also noticeable that neither the unmarried Jesus nor the unmarried Paul would have qualified for office on these terms.

Deacons

3.8–13

3.8–10 The requirements for deacons are introduced with *likewise* because they describe a similar social type. The Greek word transliterated by *deacon* means *servant*, and it is widely used in NT epistles of apostles and other church leaders (e.g. Rom. 16.1; I Cor. 3.5; Eph. 6.21; Phil. 1.1; I Thess. 3.2). It is also used in Hellenistic inscriptions of people with responsibilities to religious associations. In 4.6, it is used of Timothy. Here, it denotes a group of leaders, but again, what their particular tasks are taken to be is unclear. Unlike the overseer, the deacon is not specifically required to be a good teacher, so it is possible that deacons are elders who do not preach and teach (5.17). On the other hand, Timothy is called a servant in 4.6, and he is required to teach. It is impossible to be sure about the deacon's duties because the advice makes no link between character and role. *Dignified/reverent* is also required of women in 3.11, and of older men in Titus 2.2 (and see the noun in 2.2; 3.4). *Double-tongued* in the sense of *insincere* is found only here and in Polycarp's *Epistle to the Philippians* 5.2 in the whole of ancient Greek literature. *Not given to excessive drinking* corresponds to *sober* in the list of qualities for the overseer. It excludes over-indulgence in alcohol but does not exclude its moderate use (5.23). *Nor to money-grubbing* is also excluded for the overseer in Titus 1.7, but the word is found nowhere else in the NT. Those who teach otherwise will later be accused of using piety for gain (6.5). *The mystery* usually refers to secret rites and teachings in Hellenistic literature (e.g. Socrates, *Epistle* 27.3, see p. 117), but it was taken up by Hellenistic Jewish writers like Josephus (*Against Apion* 2.189) to refer to Judaism. In the NT, it can refer to God's hidden plan which is apprehended by believers (e.g. Mark 4.11 parr; I Cor. 2.1, 7; 4.1; 13.2; 14.2; Eph. 1.9; Col. 2.2). Here the emphasis is on the deacons' holding the mystery of *the faith*, that is, of the Christian faith as understood by the epistle. And they are to do so *with a pure/clear conscience* (cf. 1.5 *good conscience*). In the Pastorals, the language of purity is used metaphorically for ethical purity (e.g. 1.5; II Tim. 1.3; 2.22; Titus 1.15; contrast Rom. 14.20).

In order to ensure that deacons conform to these standards, the instructions state that they should be *tested first* (REB *undergo scrutiny*) and only if they prove *blameless* (REB *of unimpeachable character*; cf. Titus 1.6 of elders, I Cor. 1.8 of all believers) are they to serve. No advice is offered about the manner of this testing, whether by examination of their general conduct or through a period of probation, nor by whom, should no Pauline delegate be present in the community.

3.11 refers to the qualities which women should exhibit, also introduced by *likewise,* but whether these women are to be understood as female deacons (REB *women in this office* adds *in this office*) like Phoebe in Rom. 16.1, or as the wives of deacons is uncertain. The latter seems more likely since verse 12 returns to the subject of male deacons. In Greek, *woman* and *wife* is the same word. Male literature often caricatures women as *scandalmongers/slanderers* (e.g. Menander, 878, cf. also Titus 2.3) but II Tim. 3.3 also attributes the vice to men in the last days.

3.12 lists further qualities required of male deacons. As in the case of the overseer, deacons are also to be *the husband of one wife* and are to *manage their children and their own households well.* Encouragement is given to those who serve well by suggesting that they would *gain a good standing* (literally *step) for themselves and great confidence in the faith which is in Christ Jesus* (REB paraphrases *entitled to high standing and the right to be heard on matters of Christian faith). Step* can be understood either as rank or as a step in their progress in the faith (cf. 4.15–16). Again, these qualifications exclude unmarried men and slaves, and perhaps also women.

The focus of these instructions on social and ethical qualities means that they provide models for all male householders in the community. Moreover, the assonance and alliteration of the Greek lists would aid memory. They share with Hellenistic moral exhortation an admiration for sober, sincere and moderate men. Such characters would not use their authority for aggressive and domineering behaviour, and would be free from the vices of rashness, stupidity, greed or ascetic extremes. Our culture has inherited this conception, and we expect our leaders, whether men or women, in the churches and in society, to share these traits. But we have also inherited another tradition, found in the Gospels and in passages like I Cor. 7, which encourage the kind of dedication to God's purpose that requires people to forego both the comforts and the responsibilities of family life in order to help others in need.

The reason for and the theological grounding of these instructions

3.14–16

3.14–15 The Pauline epistles often refer to plans about future visits to communities by Paul and his delegates (e.g. Rom. 1.11; 15.24; II Cor. 12.14; 13.1). Here the expression of Paul's hope to visit Ephesus in the near future encourages the speedy implementation of his instructions, while the possibility of his delay explains the need for the epistle. The particular form of expression, *in case I am delayed*, however, is found only here and in II Peter 3.9 in the NT. This break in the flow of the epistle's advice allows a general summary of its contents: *what is proper conduct in God's household, that is, the church of the living God*. The summary also serves as theological grounding for the patriarchal structure of the church advocated in the earlier parts of the epistle. The Pastorals contain little criticism of patriarchal structures, and no suggestion that devotion to God and Christ might take precedence over family loyalty, as the Gospels and other Paulines do (e.g. Matt. 10.35–37; 12.46–50 and parr; I Cor. 7.32–35). Rather, a conservative conception of the family, ruled over by the father, is used to create a conservative, patriarchal church structure which marginalises the more egalitarian conception of the church as a brotherhood. The Greek word translated *household* also means *house*, in the sense of a building, so that the image of the church as a *pillar and bulwark*, supporting *the truth*, arises naturally.

3.16 Since *the truth* refers to the truth about God's purpose explained by the epistle's exposition of the Christian faith, as in 2.4–6, this reference is followed by a summary of that faith. It is introduced formally: *And great, confessedly, is the mystery of the piety* (REB paraphrases *And great beyond all question is the mystery of our religion*). What follows delineates what had earlier been called *the mystery of the faith*, to which deacons and all believers are encouraged to hold. The first word of the confession, however, varies among the old manuscripts that have survived. Some read *who* (REB *he*), referring to Christ, and some read *which*, referring to the mystery. The confession is expressed in a balanced, rhythmic form, through related pairs: *flesh/spirit* (cf. Rom. 1.3–6; I Peter 3.18); *angels/nations* (cf. the belief that each people is represented by an angel, Dan. 12.1); *world/glory*. There is some tension between this teaching and that of other Paulines. *Seen by angels* has no parallel in the NT unless it is implied by Phil. 2.10. In I Cor. 15.24, Christ's triumph is described as a triumph over principalities and powers, and is conceived as still future. Col. 2.15 and Eph. 3.10, however, understand Christ's triumph over principalities and powers as already accomplished. The reference to a successful Gentile mission before Christ's final taking up serves to ground that mission in Jesus' own historical ministry, as in Matt. and Mark, but not in Gal. 1–2. *Taken up/raised* uses the same expression as II Kings 2.20, about Elijah, and Acts 1.11, about Jesus, but finds no parallel in other Paulines. The confession contains no reference to Jesus' death and resurrection (contrast I Cor. 15.3–11; Phil. 2.6–11). These features, however, create less tension with other teaching in the Pastorals, in which there is only one explicit reference to Jesus' death (II Tim. 2.8–11, cf. I Tim. 2.6), never specified as crucifixion, none to principalities and powers, and according to which salvation is both a present reality and a future hope. The confession highlights Christ's universal triumph, and this perspective provides both a fitting conclusion to the teaching given so far, and the presupposition of the teaching which will follow in 4.1–5. The rhythmic, balanced form has suggested to commentators that the confession is a quotation from a liturgical source, and, if this were so, it would invite the reader's ready acceptance. But just those beliefs expressed are required for the argument at this point in the epistle, and it is possible that they were written to serve that purpose, and in a form which makes them memorable.

Notes on 3.1–16

3.1 *Here is a saying you may trust* Some manuscripts replace *sure/trust* by *human*. This reading treats the aspiration to the office of overseer as a human aspiration, not to be placed in the same category as other statements which follow the expression in the Pastorals. It is probably secondary.

The office of overseer The word, in this sense, appears only here in contemporary literature, but *overseer* is mentioned in relation to various kinds of leaders in Num 4.16; 31.14; Josephus, *Ant.* 10.53; and frequently in Greek inscriptions about men with financial responsibilities for social groups. The Pastorals, however, do not suggest that the role of the overseer is confined to financial concerns, nor even that it includes them.

3.2 *Above reproach* In the NT, only here and in 5.7 in relation to widows. But the quality is frequently recommended in Hellenistic

29

writings e.g. Dio Chrysostom 11.66; Philo, *Special Laws* 3.24. What is meant by the term is illustrated in the list of attributes which follows in the text.

Temperate /moderate Moderation or good judgment was a cardinal virtue in Greek philosophy. The noun, the adjective and the adverb are found frequently in the Pastorals but nowhere in other Paulines (2.9, 15; II Tim. 1.7; Titus 1.8; 2.2, 4, 5). Their use suggests the influence of Hellenistic philosophy. The Pastorals, like other Hellenistic writings, present the moderate person as an ideal type.

3.6 *Puffed up with conceit* cf. II Tim. 3.4 of vicious people in the last days. Note that a different verb is used in I Cor. 8.1.

3.15 *The church* Note the singular and cf. Deut. 31.30; Judg. 20.2; I Cor. 12.28.

Living God cf. II Kings 19.4, 16; Rom. 9.26 quoting Hos. 1.10; II Cor. 3.3; I Thess. 1.9.

Pillar Gal. 2.9 uses the image to refer to James, Cephas and John, cf. Rev. 3.12.

Bulwark is found only here in the NT but the related adjective is used in I Cor. 15.58; Col. 1.23.

3.16 *Confessedly/ beyond all question* cf. IV Macc. 6.31.

Piety/religion This disposition characterises devotion to God and his purpose. It is repeatedly recommended in the Pastorals, the noun occurring here and in 2.2; 4.7–8; 6.3, 5–6, 11; II Tim. 3.5; Titus 1.1; with the verb in I Tim. 5.4 and the adverb in II Tim. 3.12; Titus 2.12. It is never used in other Paulines, and occurs in the NT outside the Pastorals only in Acts and II Peter. It was considered to be one of the cardinal virtues by Hellenistic writers and was given even greater emphasis by Jewish Hellenistic writers like Philo and Josephus, as by the Pastorals, because they understand ethics as theological ethics (e.g. Plato, *Republic* 615C; Diodorus Siculus 19.7; Epictetus, *Enchiridion* 31; Philo, *Posterity of Cain* 81; Josephus, *Ant.* 18.117). Ancient Greek had no word for *religion* as we do.

Apostasies of later times refuted in advance
4.1–5

The confession of Christ's present universal triumph in 3.16 provides a reason for not forsaking *the faith by giving heed to deceitful spirits and teachings of demons* (REB paraphrases *surrender their minds to subversive spirits and demon-inspired doctrines*). The assertion that the *Spirit explicitly warns* is not justified by a quotation from Scripture or any other source, but could refer to the common Jewish apocalyptic belief that apostasy would precede God's final eschatological judgment (e.g. Dan. 12.1; I Enoch 6–11; cf. Eph. 6.11–12; II Thess. 2.1–12; II Tim. 3.1–9). In this way, what is believed about the last days mirrors earlier descriptions of God's people's infidelity before God's deliverance (e.g. Gen. 6–9; Judges; Isa. 40–55; I and II Macc.). So here, in the later days, even believers are expected to fall under the influence of deceitful spirits and teachings of demons, and, through the hypocrisy of false statements, to become people whose conscience is *seared* or *cauterised*. In 1.19–20, Hymenaeus and Alexander are said to have been delivered to Satan to learn not to slander, because they had rejected conscience. These people who would appear in later times, however, are understood to be in a worse state because their conscience would be completely insensitive, offering no guard against wrong actions. The wrong actions are then specified: they would *forbid marriage and insist on abstinence from foods.* Hellenistic writings, including medical writings, from the end of the first century CE onwards, increasingly advocated chastity in marriage and a simple diet, but only some philosophical movements advocated celibacy and vegetarianism (e.g. Philostratus' account of the life and teachings of the first century CE religious leader, Apollonius of Tyana). I Tim. formally counters the practice of abstinence from foods by asserting that *God created foods to be enjoyed with thanksgiving by believers who have come to knowledge of the truth.* The point is emphasised by further explanation and the language echoes that of Gen. 1.31 and Ps. 33.6: *because everything that God has created is*

31

good, and nothing is to be rejected provided it is received with thanksgiving.
Finally, another explanation is added: *for it is consecrated by the saying
of God and prayer* (REB paraphrases *for it is then made holy by God's
word and by prayer*). The reference to God's saying may be to Gen.
1.31. I Cor. 10.23–31 argues against abstaining from foods offered to
idols, except out of consideration for others, on similar grounds, that
the earth is the Lord's and that food should therefore be received
with thanks (cf. Col. 2.20–23). But this passage in I Tim. does not
suggest that future encouragement of abstinence from food would be
urged because of qualms about food offered to idols, nor because of
concern to avoid food forbidden by the Jewish Scriptures. Rather, it
understands the ascetic practices to arise from an implied denial of
the goodness of material existence, and so insists that God creates
the world and that it is good. Although the practice of forbidding
marriage is not formally refuted, the assertion of the goodness of
God's creation and the echoes of Genesis 1, which also enjoins
marriage and bearing children, implies the error of such teaching.

This passage expects these evil teachings to arise *in later times,* not
in the present. But commentators like Dibelius-Conzelmann,
Houlden and Hanson, who regard the Pastorals as pseudonymous,
and who date them at the beginning of the second century, suggest
that these *later times* represent the present situation of the actual
church addressed. The early second century Christian 'heretic',
Marcion, for example, advocated ascetic practices, and second
century Christian Gnosticism denied that God creates the world. But
centuries before, Plato had denied that God creates the world (e.g.in
Timaeus). Since no connexion is made in the epistle between the later
times and Timothy's future experience, the expected bad teachings,
and the practices they enjoin, are best understood as the antithesis of
the positive teaching of the epistle, which favours marriage (3.4, 12;
5.14) and endorses the moderate enjoyment of wine (5.23), indeed,
advocates moderation in all things (2.9, 15; 3.2; II Tim. 1.7; Titus 1.8;
2.2, 4, 5). Asceticism is presented as an immoderate perversion.
Moreover, reference to what would happen in the later times serves
to encourage Timothy to safeguard the epistle's teaching and to pass
it on to others (4.6, 16; 6.20), so that it could be used against probable
perversions.

In countering asceticism, the epistle reaffirms the biblical tradition
of the goodness of God's creation. Material existence is represented
as beneficent, not threatening to human well-being, if a moderate
lifestyle is pursued by God's grace. But the epistle also recognises the

existence of evil spiritual beings, opposed to the Creator God: Satan (1.20; 5.15), and spirits and demons (4.1), and some believers are understood to be liable to their influence. Nevertheless, such spirits are called *deceitful* because real power is recognised as belonging to God (cf. II Tim. 1.7–8; 3.5), and because God's agent, Jesus, is believed to have triumphed universally (3.16). The Pastorals, however, while representing humans as sinners in need of salvation, contain no further reflections on the problem of evil, no sense that Creation was subjected to futility and is waiting for the revealing of the sons of God (Rom. 8). To contemporary readers, many of whom are concerned with human over-exploitation of the world's resources, they appear to be unduly optimistic. Their stress, however, on the importance of people's moderation in personal relations and their general condemnation of greed could be extended to avoid some of the excesses of contemporary living.

Notes on 4.1–5

4.1 *Subversive/deceitful spirits* is literally *spirits that lead astray*. II John 7b identifies 'the deceiver' and 'the antichrist'. Nowhere else are *deceitful spirits* mentioned, but II Thess. 2.11 refers to God's sending a *strong delusion* to make people believe what is false; cf. II Tim. 3.13; Titus 3.3.
Demons The LXX associates demons and idolatry (e.g. Deut. 32.17; Baruch 4.7) as does Paul in I Cor. 10.20–21. The assertion that idolatry leads people astray is common in the Jewish Scriptures (e.g. Isa. 46.8; Wisd. 12.24) and is expressed by Paul in Rom. 1.18–23. The Pastorals, however, never expressly mention idolatry.

Encouragement for Timothy to pursue his teaching responsibilities and advice about how he should exemplify his teaching in practice
4.6–16

4.6–7 *By offering such advice to the brotherhood* requires Timothy to pass on the teaching contained in the epistle to all the members of the believing community, called *brothers* because they are conceived as a surrogate family under God's fatherhood (1.2). The androcentrism of the text means that sisters are mentioned only rarely (e.g. 5.2). Encouragement is offered by asserting that, in doing so, Timothy *will prove to be a good servant of Christ Jesus.* Jesus, the Messiah, is to be served well by those who believe in him. *A good servant* is then defined as someone *nurtured in the precepts of the faith and of the good teaching which you have followed,* that is, the teaching represented by the contents of the epistle, metaphorically conceived as food for life. Mentioning that Timothy already has experience of following this teaching confirms his present status as a good servant, and exhorts him to continue in the same manner. An alternative way, already characterised in 1.3–4, is now recalled in order to reinforce the positive teaching through a negative example of what to avoid: *have nothing to do with profane or superstitious myths, mere old wives' tales.* The content of these myths is not specified, nor are they refuted. A conventional derogatory description is used to make them contemptible in the eyes of the reader.

4.8–9 By contrast, nourished on the food of the approved teaching, Timothy is to *train* himself *in piety* (REB paraphrases *keep yourself in training for the practice of religion*). The language of physical training is used metaphorically to capture the sense of hard and steady practice

34

required in the religious and ethical sphere, as in sport. The metaphor was commonly used in Hellenistic philosophical literature (e.g. Epictetus 2.18.27; 3.3.14). Its metaphorical force is made clear by the following verse: *for while the training of the body brings limited benefit, the benefits of piety are without limit, since it holds out promise for the present life and for the life to come.* This image of training emphasises the responsibility of the individual, since, as in bodily training, no one else can undertake the spiritual training required. And this appeal to the individual, which will be repeated in 4.15–16, is taken up from Hellenistic philosophy. It is, however, linked with Christian belief by the assertion that it holds out promise not only for the present life but for the life to come. As well as the belief that God's present creation is good (4.4), the Pastorals also look forward to a future eschatological transformation, when believers would receive eternal life (1.16; 6.12; Titus I.2; 3.7). Here, the contrast is expressed as *present life* and *life to come*, expressions found nowhere else in the NT. More often, present life is called *the present age* (6.17; II Tim. 4.10; Titus 2.12), which implies a future age. In 1.17, God had been called *King of Ages*, recognising his sovereignty over both the present and the future age.

The hope of eternal life for believing human beings at the eschaton, however, implies that there is something wrong with present mortal human existence, even that of believers. In 1.15, the purpose of Jesus' life was said to be the saving of sinners, but nowhere in the Pastorals is an explicit connexion made between sin and death. The belief that sin brought death, however, has to be assumed in order to make sense of this teaching about eschatological eternal life. That sin brought death was a belief of Hellenistic Judaism (Wisd. 2.23–24; II Esd. 3.7), and it is explicitly expressed in Rom. 5.12, 14; 6.23; I Cor. 15.21–22 (cf. James 1.15). The Pastorals take it for granted. That piety holds out promise for the present life and for the life to come is confirmed by the assertion: *here is a saying you may trust, one that merits full acceptance* (see 1.15).

4.10 This perspective is then used to justify Paul's and Timothy's hard work: *this is why we labour and struggle.* The variant reading: *suffer reproach,* could be original, since *struggle* is combined with *labour* in Col. 1.19 and that passage could have influenced the reading here. Yet *struggle* fits better with the image of training. In view of the promise of eternal life, present toil among Gentiles seems worthwhile. Hence, this perspective is re-emphasised in different words:

because we have set our hope on the living God, who is the Saviour of all people, especially believers. Hope is an appropriate disposition for those who look forward to the life to come (cf. 6.17; Titus 1.2; 2.13; 3.7; Rom. 8.24–25; I Cor. 13.7). Earlier teaching is summarised in this statement: that God is Saviour (1.1) and desires all people to be saved through Christ Jesus (2.3–4). *Believers* have already affirmed that belief and, according to the epistle, should already be expressing their belief in good works engendered by God's grace.

4.11–13 Timothy is therefore urged to *insist on these things in your teaching* (4.11). But his teaching should also be exemplified in his conduct. As in the Jewish tradition, so also in the Hellenistic tradition, and in the contemporary Western tradition, people are respected only if they practise what they preach. *Let no one despise you as young* (cf. I Cor. 16.11) criticises a common assumption of patriarchal societies, that youth should defer to the experience of age. To a large extent, the epistle endorses this common view, both in the form of the letter itself, in which an older man, Paul, instructs a younger man, Timothy, and in its support for the rule of elders over the community (4.14; 5.17–22). Yet Timothy is made an exception in one respect. He is to teach others, even to discipline elders, in spite of his youth, and is to provide an example for all believers, whatever their age, *in speech and behaviour, in love, faith and purity.* I Cor. 13.13 associates love and faith with hope, and in 13.2 faith is treated as a disposition, as it is here. The word translated *purity,* however, occurs only here and 5.2 in the NT. Taken in context, it seems to refer to a moral purity which would not find expression in the extremes of asceticism (4.3). *Until I arrive* reminds Timothy of Paul's expected visit (3.14), but also makes clear that Timothy acts as Paul's agent only during his absence, and that he would be held responsible for the successful completion of the task Paul sets him. He is to *devote* himself *to public reading, to exhortation and to teaching.* What is to be read is not specified. It could refer either to the public reading of the Jewish Scriptures, a quotation from which is used to support teaching in 5.17, and an allusion to which had been made in 2.13–15, or to the public reading of the epistle itself, since the final grace is expressed with *you* plural (6.21; cf. Col. 4.16; I Thess. 5.27). In either case, we can infer that community assemblies are to be concerned not only with prayers (2.1–2, 8) but also with reading, exhortation and teaching.

4.14–16   Timothy's special position as an authoritative teacher, in spite of his youth, is now explained by the command that he should *not neglect the charisma* or *spiritual endowment which is in you*. In other words, Timothy's leadership is conceived as charismatic, as a gift from God (cf. I Cor. 12.4–11). Ultimately, therefore, his standing and the possibility of his training in the faith and teaching others is seen as the expression of God's special gift to him. Moreover, the text notes when the charisma was given to him: *which was given to you when, under (the guidance of) prophecy, the council of elders laid their hands on you*. The phraseology suggests that Timothy's charisma was recognised through prophecy, though through which prophet is not mentioned, and that this recognition was endorsed by the council of elders' laying on of hands. For the practice of laying on hands in relation to community responsibilities, cf. 5.22; Num. 27.18–23; Deut. 34.9; Acts 6.6; 13.3. In II Tim. 1.6, Timothy's charisma is associated with Paul's laying on of hands. Here, the reference to the council of elders functions as a reminder that Timothy's standing had already been acknowledged by the leaders of the community at Ephesus. This is the only reference to a Christian *council of elders* in the NT. A Jewish council of elders is mentioned in Jewish sources and in Luke 22.66 and Acts 22.5 (see Campbell, 1994).

In the light of this reminder to Timothy of his receipt of the charisma from God, the subject of his training is resumed. He is urged to *practise these things,* to be *in them* (REB paraphrases *Make these matters your business, make them your absorbing interest*). Moreover, practice is said to bring *progress,* a notion already taken up in Hellenistic Jewish writings from Hellenistic philosophical literature (cf. Diog. L. 4.50; Ecclus 51.17; Josephus, *Ant.* 4.59; Phil. 1.25). By making progress, Timothy is assured that he would provide an example for others to follow: *your progress may be plain to all.* Hence, Timothy is to *keep a close watch* both on himself and on the teaching, and he is to *persevere.* A final encouragement is provided by the assurance that: *by so doing you will save both yourself and your hearers.* The teaching and its practice are said to have saving significance because they make known the salvation which God gives (4.10). This section, therefore, creates a portrait of a good teacher who would provide a model for others, in his speech, in his lifestyle and in his progress, and Timothy is urged to instantiate the portrait.

Notes on 4.6–16

4.6 *Insist on* (REB *Offering such advice*) The verb, in its middle form, is found only here in the NT; cf. Plato, *Charmides* 155D.

4.7 *Old wives' tales* The adjective occurs only here in the NT, but it was a common derogatory epithet in Hellenistic literature; e.g. Strabo 1.2.3; Epictetus 2.16.39. It implies the kind of contempt for what older women say which was as common among men in the Hellenistic world as it is today.

4.10 *Especially believers* Skeat, 1979, argues that *especially* is better translated *that is to say or in other words*. See also 5.8, 17; II Tim. 4.13; Titus 1.10.

Advice about various groups within the believing community
5.1–6.19

Older and younger men and women
5.1–2

After many exhortations to Timothy about what he should teach and how he should practice what he taught, consideration is now given to the manner in which he should relate to groups within the believing community, distinguished by age and gender. So Timothy is *not to be harsh with an older man* but is *to appeal to him as a father*. That Timothy's manner to older men is actually specified reflects a felt awareness of the difficulty any younger man would experience in a patriarchal society (cf. 4.11–14). His manner towards a younger man and an older woman is merely suggested by the metaphors *brother* and *mother*, but his manner towards a younger woman is indicated in more detail, *in all purity* (cf. 4.12), since, again, some difficulty is assumed. Here *purity* probably conveys the nuance *sexual purity*. Titus 2.2–6 indicates what Titus should teach to each of these same groups. These divisions by age and gender reflect the structure of a patriarchal society, in which older men would have authority over younger men and all women, younger men would have authority over women, and older women would have authority over younger women (see 2.11–14). II Tim. 2.24–25 and 4.2 will provide more detailed advice about Timothy's manner of teaching.

Widows

5.3–16

The support of widows by the covenant community is enjoined in the Jewish Scriptures (e.g. Deut. 25.20). By contrast, Graeco-Roman

39

literature encourages no community welfare for widows, but leaves the responsibility for their support to families. Roman widows from rich families could live secure lives because their dowries would be returned to them, but few widows came from rich families. NT literature suggests that Christian communities adopted the teaching of the Jewish Scriptures (cf. Acts 6.1; I Cor. 7.39–40). This section of I Tim., however, distinguishes both real widows and selected or enrolled widows from other widows. Are the real widows to be identified with the enrolled widows? The REB assumes that they are, and adds the word *enrol* to 5.3.

5.3–8   The command to *honour widows who are real widows* involves not only according them respect, but also providing them with financial support. These *real widows*, however, are distinguished from widows with surviving descendants: *if a widow has children or grandchildren, let them first learn to behave piously to their own household and to give back a return to their forebears* (REB paraphrases *they should learn as their first duty to show loyalty to the family and so repay what they owe to their parents and grandparents*) . This behaviour is encouraged, both by describing it as pious, and by the explanatory clause: *for that has God's approval*. A *real widow* is identified by repeating what had already been suggested, though in a different way – she is *alone* – and by describing the kind of piety which should characterise her life: *who has set her hope on God and continues in supplications and prayers night and day* (cf. Luke 2.37; the REB paraphrases *puts all her trust in God, and regularly, night and day, attends the meetings for prayer and worship*). Moreover, she should be *above reproach* (compare 3.2 of the overseer), in distinction from a widow who is *self-indulgent* and who is pronounced *as good as dead*. Community support for real widows, left alone, therefore, is made conditional on their acceptable behaviour. The advice then returns to warn any descendant of a widow that failure to support her amounts to denying *the faith*, making him even *worse than an unbeliever*. As throughout the Pastorals, people are expected to express their belief in good works, and this strong warning is designed to succeed if the earlier exhortation that they support family widows failed.

5.9–10   Do these verses further define the real widows, or do they refer to another group of widows? The second alternative seems to make better sense of the details. The qualifications listed for those widows who are to be enrolled would exclude some widows without descendants and seems to include widows with children: *not less than sixty years old, the wife of one husband, a reputation for good deeds,* including having *brought up children, shown hospitality* (see the adjective in 3.3 in the list of qualities for the overseer), *washed the feet of the saints* (REB paraphrases *God's people*), *supported those in distress.* These characteristics are summarised as *devoted herself to every good work* (REB paraphrases *in short by doing good at every opportunity*). Probably, *hospitality and washing the feet of the saints* are to be taken together to refer to the good deed of accomodating travelling delegates or missionaries. Verses 11–12 exclude younger widows from enrolment and imply that those enlisted take a vow not to remarry, a vow younger widows are expected to break. That some widows are to be formally enrolled and their good deeds for the community recognised probably implies that they would receive financial support from the community too. This group of women, and the woman mentioned below in 5.16, are the only female members of the community who are recognised as serving the community as a whole, rather than simply their own families. This contrasts with the impression created by Rom. 16; I Cor. 7 and 11, and Phil. 4.2–3, passages which recognise a much larger group of women as Paul's fellow-workers and prophets.

5.11–15   Further reasons are given for excluding younger widows from enrolment: they would learn to become *idle, going from house to house, gossips and busybodies, speaking of things better left unspoken.* This is a typical Hellenistic caricature of women free from male control (contrast I Cor. 7.15, 25–26, 34, 40). The caricature is used to justify the advice which follows: *I would have younger widows marry, have children, manage their households, and give the enemy no occasion to revile.* In other words, younger widows are to be brought under the control of men through remarriage, so that the *enemy,* probably a critical outsider, could not revile believers for allowing them to remain unmarried. Following the advice would mean that these women, if they were widowed a second time, could never be enrolled, since enrolment is conditional on their being the wife of one husband. Moreover, the advice is buttressed by suggesting that some younger widows had already strayed after Satan, presumably by becoming idlers, gossips and busybodies. The instruction about all younger widows is based on the bad behaviour of some. In the next section, however, the role of elders is not abolished because some elders act badly. Furthermore, we never find in Hellenistic literature the suggestion that men should marry, have children and manage their households so that they would avoid becoming idlers, gossips and busybodies, although men are as prone to these vices as women are. And what is so striking about this denigration of women (see also 2.11–15) is the contrast it affords with the confidence Paul expresses in women free from male control, who signify their devotion to God in the service of communities, according to Romans and I Corinthians. The Pastorals allow women so little opportunity for these kinds of service that most women without family responsibilities are left with nothing to do.

5.16 suggests that there might be a believing woman whose means would allow her to undertake the care of widows, whether members of her family or not, and that this would alleviate the financial burden on the rest of the community (cf. Acts 9.36–43). Actually, this concern to relieve the community of a financial burden seems to underlie all the advice about the treatment of widows in this section. The qualifications for counting as a real widow and those required for enrolled widows, and the severe warning issued against descendants who do not support their widows, all tend in the same direction: they free the community from the responsibility of supporting most widows. The advice contains no hint of the generosity advocated in other parts of the NT (e.g. Matt. 5.40–42 par; I Cor. 13.3). Moreover, this advice about community support, or lack of support, of vulnerable women contrasts with the advice about the financial support of male elders in the next section.

Good and bad elders

5.17–22

5.17–18 The older men, about whom advice is given in this section, are to be understood as elders who exercised a ruling function (cf. 4.14; Titus 1.5; and contrast 5.1). In an ancient patriarchal society, it is taken to be self-evident that leaders should come from the group of older, experienced men. That society did not change at the astonishing speed of contemporary Western society, so experience could more usefully be passed from one generation to another. The teaching recommends that *elders who rule well* (REB paraphrases *who give good service as leaders),* especially those involved in *preaching and teaching,* should be recognised as worthy of a *double honour,* that is, a double financial honorarium (REB *double stipend).* This may mean double the honorarium given to real and enrolled widows. Elders not occupied with preaching and teaching would be concerned with less time-consuming matters, perhaps things like selecting widows for enrolment. The emphasis on preaching and teaching reflects a major concern of the epistle. The double honorarium would compensate the preachers and teachers for the time spent away from their livelihood. The advice is justified by quoting the same passage in Deut. 25.4 as that used to warrant the support of apostles in I Cor. 9.9, but I Tim. exactly reproduces the Septuagint text, whereas I Cor. does not. This is the only explicit quotation from the Jewish Scriptures in the Pastorals, but there are allusions to the Scriptures elsewhere (e.g. 2.13–14; 5.19). The advice is also endorsed by the commonplace: *the worker earns his pay* (cf. Matt. 10.10 par).

5.19–21 Elders, however, might be subject to criticism, and further exhortation to Timothy suggests ways in which criticism should be handled. The requirement for *two or three witnesses* to sustain an accusation echoes Deut. 17.6; 19.15; or I Cor. 13.1, although those passages concern all members of the community, not just elders. The text recognises, however, that some elders might be persistent sinners and suggests that they should be rebuked or convicted *in the presence of all to put fear into the others. All* and *the others* could refer either to all the elders or to the whole community assembly. Similar advice, though in different vocabulary, is given in Deut. 19.20. Timothy's impartial judgment, which, in a patriarchal society, could prove difficult for a younger man in relation to an older leader (cf. 4.12), is buttressed by reminding him of the theological context of all his actions: *before God, Christ Jesus and the elect angels.* Christ's universal triumph had already been highlighted in 3.16, and now God's and his presence in the community are acknowledged. The references to Christ's past appearing and his future appearing, therefore, do not preclude the sense of Christ's continuing presence. Timothy's impartiality is also encouraged by a solemn charge.

In contrast with other Paulines (e.g. I Cor. 5; Gal. 6.1–6), it is noticeable that the Pastorals expect Timothy or Titus alone to take disciplinary action and to sort out difficulties in the local community (cf. Titus 3.10–11). It is never suggested that he should call a community assembly so that the community is encouraged to exercise discipline, nor do these epistles ever express confidence in the community's ability to do so. And never do the Pastorals acknowledge or urge the delegates to acknowledge that the believing community as a whole provides an example of fidelity for others to follow (contrast I Thess. 1.3–10; 2.13–14, 19–20; 3.6–10; 4.9–10). All this is consonant with the Pastorals' emphasis, not on the whole community as the body of Christ, but on the leadership of Timothy, Titus and the local male elders, overseer(s) and deacons in a church conceived on the model of a patriarchal household (3.15).

5.22 Finally, in this section, advice is given about how to avoid further difficulties with elders. Timothy is exhorted not to be *overhasty in the laying on of hands*. We gather, therefore, that elders were also acknowledged through the laying on of hands, as Timothy had been acknowledged by the council of elders (4.14). Here, Timothy's responsibility to appoint elders is assumed, as in the appointment of suitable overseer(s) and deacons in 3.1–13 (cf. Titus 1.5), where similar caution is also encouraged (3.6, 10). Moreover, the earlier charge against partiality in judging recalcitrant elders is reinforced with a command not to *participate in the sins of others* (REB paraphrases *you may find yourself implicated in other people's misdeeds*). Failure to rebuke bad elders is construed as participation in their sins. Hence the final injunction: *keep yourself pure* (cf. 4.12; REB *above reproach*).

A little wine

5.23

A moment's severity is counterbalanced by the expression of personal concern for Timothy's health, a common topic in Hellenistic letters. *A little wine* suggests the moderation between asceticism (cf. 4.3) and drunkeness (cf. 3.3, 8). Timothy's ill-health invites sympathy, and highlights the difficulty of his work as a travelling delegate. No reference is made, however, to the possiblility of miraculous healing (contrast I Cor. 12.9, 28 and compare II Tim. 4.20). In the ancient world, wine was considered to be a useful medicine (e.g. Plutarch, *Advice about keeping well* 19, *Mor.* 132B).

Judgment

5.24–25

These remarks could refer to the final eschatological judgment (so e.g Kelly, Dibelius-Conzelmann, Hanson), or they could continue the subject of verse 22, discouraging Timothy's hasty appointment of elders and encouraging his impartial rebuke of those who continue to sin. The second suggestion would make better sense of the reference to *sins* (REB *offences*) and *good deeds* only becoming apparent after some time.

Slaves

6.1–2

6.1   Slaves had not specifically been mentioned as members of the households of overseer or deacon in chapter 3, but this final chapter of the epistle includes reference both to slaves and to the wealthy who would own them (6.17–19). Elsewhere in the NT, household codes include instructions about the behaviour of slaves and their believing masters (Eph. 6.9; Col. 4.1), but, like I Peter 2.18–25, the Pastorals contain no instructions for masters, in spite of the acknowledgement that some slaves would have believing masters (6.2; cf. Titus 2.9–10). In an urban setting like Ephesus, slaves would have worked in administration, in commerce, in workshops, in entertainment, as prostitutes in brothels and on the streets, and as household servants of the rich. Slaves were not free to determine either what they did or when they did it. They also had no control over their own persons and might be required to provide sexual services for their masters and mistresses (e.g. Petronius' *Satyricon* 75.11; Horace's *Satires* 1.2.116–119). They were not free to keep themselves pure as Timothy had been urged to do (4.12; 5.2). They could be cruelly punished by beatings or starvation, even by death. Slaves were treated as 'living tools.' They were bought and sold. They could not legally marry, and any children born to them might be exposed or, if they were brought up, might be sold elsewhere. In any case, any slave children born in the household would belong to the master. Slaves' treatment depended on the disposition and whims of their masters. Nevertheless, some slaves were promised manumission by their masters as an incentive for good service, and this was most commonly effected when the master died, through a stipulation in his will. Their freedom, however, would not include that of their children or of the persons they regarded as their spouses. Otherwise, slaves were inherited along with other property. This is the social context in which advice about the appropriate behaviour of believing slaves is given to Timothy.

The instruction insists that slaves, whether of unbelieving or believing masters, are to *consider their masters as worthy of all honour or respect*, that is, they are to regard them as worthy just because they are masters and irrespective of their moral character and behaviour, or the demands they make on the believing slaves. I Peter 2.18–25 more realistically recognises that slaves might have cruel masters and might be made to suffer horrible punishments for doing what is right as well as for any misdemeanours. Christ's suffering is held up as a model for them of patient endurance, and assurance is given of Christ's just judgment. These perspectives are lacking in the Pastorals. I Tim.'s demand that slaves should abandon their own religious and moral insight in order to regard even bad masters as worthy of honour is unreasonable. And the advice is given *so that the name of God and the teaching may not be brought into disrepute*. Believing slaves who were guilty of bad actions might cause the kind of slander which it is not unreasonable to suggest should be avoided, but what about believing slaves who refused to perform actions they considered irreligious or immoral, like those excluded by the general paraenetic of the epistle? A bad master might slander the faith for such a refusal, but would it not have been better to encourage the slave in such a stand, as I Peter does?

6.2   goes on to prohibit slaves from treating believing masters dis- respectfully because they are *brothers*. That is, all members of the believing community are regarded as brothers (cf. 4.6). Nevertheless, slaves are to continue serving believing masters. The reason given for this is ambiguous in the Greek. It could refer either to slave owners or to the slaves themselves as *believers* and *beloved* (REB para- phrases *one with them in faith and love*). The reference to *brothers* suggests that believing slaves might regard themselves as honoured in the same way as free people within the community, as I Cor. 7.21–23; Gal. 3.28; 5.1 encourage believers to do. They might even have expected to be given their freedom by believing masters, so that they would become brothers in reality, not just in name. The first century Jewish writer, Philo, claims that Jewish Essenes 'denounce the owners of slaves, not merely for outraging the law of equality, but also for their impiety in annulling the statute of nature, who like a mother has borne and reared all alike as genuine brothers, not in name only but in reality' (*Every good man is free* 79). This shows that the expectation was not unthinkable in the first century world. But this passage in I Tim. makes it clear that believing slaves of believing masters are brothers in name only. Elsewhere, the epistle insists that beliefs should find expression in the practice of good deeds, but not here in the case of believing masters. Also elsewhere, there are allusions to the Jewish Scriptures, but there is never an allusion to God's saving Hebrew slaves from Egypt, nor to the commands to release debt slaves in the seventh year (Deut. 15.12–15; see also Lev 25). The Pastorals also assume that slave owners were not required to free their slaves when they joined the believing community. Such a requirement would have been neither illegal nor anachronistic. Pagans sometimes freed their slaves. The matter was entirely in the slave owners' hands. Moreover, although community support for some widows and elders is encouraged (5.3, 17), no suggestion is made that the community should purchase the freedom of believing slaves, not even on the grounds that only freedom would allow slaves of pagan masters to practise the religious and ethical demands of the epistle. Once again, the patriarchal structure of society, even in this, its cruellest manifestation, is endorsed. Timothy is urged to teach and exhort requirements which helped to support Christian ownership of slaves until the nineteenth century.

A return to the subject of those who teach differently and the contrast between their lives and a life of self-sufficiency

6.3–10

6.3–5 The person who *teaches otherwise* is defined as someone who does not *devote himself to the healthy precepts of our Lord Jesus Christ and the teaching which accords with piety* (REB *good religious teaching*). That is, their teaching is represented as the antithesis of the teaching the epistle advocates, and once more a medical metaphor highlights its usefulness. *Precepts of our Lord Jesus Christ* does not refer to Jesus' own teaching but to the teaching about him. Just as Hellenistic philosophical literature caricatures the teaching of others, so does the Pastorals. Karris' article (1973) demonstrates how conventional the caricatures are, in accusing others of verbal disputes and quibbles, of ignorance, of deceiving, of failing to practice what they preach, and of teaching for financial rewards (see the notes for details). Nevertheless, Karris understands the Pastorals' teaching as polemical, directed against actual historical opponents. But Fiore's study (1986, chapter 8), which also draws attention to the conventional nature of the Pastorals' negative caricatures, suggests that their function is not polemical but hortatory. These caricatures serve as contrasts to the descriptions of healthy teaching and the behaviour it is said to engender. The negative highlights the positive. This explains why the content of alternative teaching is never cited and never refuted, as it is in other Paulines (e.g. Rom. 1–4, 9–11; Gal. 1–4; I Cor.). It is merely characterised in general negative terms. This also explains why those commentators (e.g. Dibelius-Conzelmann) who try to define an historical group of 'heretics' on the basis of the Pastorals' caricatures, as Judaising Gnostics, have to admit that the portrait corresponds to no group known to Christian history. Brief contrasting portraits have always been found useful in hortatory literature. Moreover, the philosophical arguments of Plato and Aristotle had convinced people that the virtues form a unity. For example, people cannot truly be just without courage, good judgment and temperance. Similarly, single vices were perceived always to be associated with other vices. The Pastorals share these views and present contrasting portraits which associate many virtues or many vices. We are inclined to view our behaviour and that of others as the expression of mixtures of virtues and vices. Of course, the Pastorals and other Hellenistic exhortation recognise the imperfections of individuals in their encouragement of people to pursue the virtues and to make progress, until virtuous behaviour becomes habitual. Where we differ from these ancient writings, however, is in our painful consciousness of the dangers, when caricatures are used as excuses for ostracising or even persecuting actual social groups.

6.6–10   The final clause of the caricature, *thinking that piety should yield dividends,* allows the exploration of a more adequate understanding of the gain to be expected from piety, just as the earlier suggestion that others wanted to be teachers of the law allowed a discussion about the true value of the law (1.7–11). *Contentment* or *self-sufficiency* was the most valued of Stoic and Cynic virtues (e.g. Zeno the Stoic 1.46; Diog. L. 10.130). In Stoicism, it represents the serenity achieved by a rational understanding and the subjugation of the passions, whatever the circumstances, whether in wealth or poverty. It expresses the central concern of Stoicism's rational cosmology and anthropology. But it fits less obviously into the theological ethics of the Pastorals, according to which the transcendent God saves people from ignorance and sin through his human agent, Christ Jesus (1.15; 2.5–6). In II Cor. 9.8, self-sufficiency is integrated into Christian theological belief by positing God as its source. Again, in Phil. 4.11, where the corresponding adjective is used, it forms part of a Christian theological perspective through the acknowledgement 'I can do all things in him who strengthens me'. Elsewhere in the Pastorals too, Hellenistic virtues are integrated into Christian beliefs. But in this passage we find no mention of either God or Christ. It is particularly strange that no mention is made of Jesus' simple lifestyle. The teaching is that of Hellenistic ethics, adopted without reflection. Among educated people in the Graeco-Roman world, *self-sufficiency* was assumed to be essential for human well-being, just as among many in contemporary Western society 'authenticity' seems essential, and Christians sometimes advocate it without wondering how it fits with their theological and anthropological beliefs. So, here in I Tim., Stoic *self-sufficiency* is explained in Stoic terms: *for we brought nothing into the world, (it is certain or true) that we can take nothing out, but, if we have food and clothing, let us rest content* (cf. Seneca, *Ep. Mor.* 102.25; Job 1.23; Philo, *Special Laws* 1.294–5). The barest human essentials are considered an adequate basis for piety with self-sufficiency (cf. Diog. L. 6.105; 10.131). The same point is confirmed by depicting its opposite: *those who want to be rich fall into temptation, into a snare, and into many foolish and harmful desires which plunge people into ruin and destruction.* This desire for wealth is perceived as so corrupting that the teaching can be summarised: *the love of money is the root of all evil.* Hence, *in pursuit of it, some have wandered from the faith and pierced themselves with many pangs* (REB paraphrases *spiked themselves on many a painful thorn*). In this way, the description is brought back to the topic of those who teach differently and suppose that piety is a means of financial gain.

For anyone living in contemporary Britain, this description of the love of money and its corrupting effects seems to depict aspects of present experience. In the 1980s, the desire for great wealth was lauded as a virtue, not a vice, and now people are encouraged to bet on the national lottery in order to become millionaires. Social workers and church ministers are reporting on the growing numbers of betting addicts who are being brought to penury and desperation. Even some Christian evangelists have been exposed as money-grubbers. Moreover, social institutions are required to evaluate all activities in terms of financial cost benefits rather than in terms of good practice, making corruption difficult to resist. The teaching of I Tim. is directed to individuals, but social and political institutions also have the power to create an ethos in which greed is encouraged and value is tested in terms of money alone. Countering such an ethos requires a vision of a more just and loving community, and an attempt to bring it about, which the Pastorals encourage with the help of God's grace through Christ Jesus.

Verner's study (1983) points out that this teaching in I Tim. criticises the desire for money and does not criticise inherited wealth. Hence, he suggests that it implicitly endorses the power of those who were already rich by excluding those who might become rivals by gaining wealth. But the depiction of self-sufficiency positively encourages a simple rather than a luxurious life, and defines a piety which is open to the poor. Moreover, as Kidd's study (1990) successfully argues, the power of the wealthy is not simply endorsed by the teaching in 6.17–19 (see below).

What Timothy should pursue

6.11–16

6.11   Once again, the lifestyle recommended to Timothy forms a contrast with that of people who teach differently. The description of Moses in Deut. 33.1 is taken up as a form of address to Timothy : *man of God* (cf. II Tim. 3.17), and he is to *flee from* or *shun* the vices just described. Rather, he is to *pursue* virtue, a common metaphor in Hellenistic exhortation, which we also find in Hellenistic Jewish writings and the Paulines (e.g. Josephus, *Ant.* 6.263; Rom. 9.31–32). *Justice*, as in Hellenistic philosophy, is treated as a cardinal virtue (cf. II Tim. 2.22; 3.16), and Pauline teaching about justification by faith is ignored (contrast Rom. 3.21; 9.31–32; Gal. 3.6). We have inherited this Greek tradition, and we also treat *justice* as a central concern of personal and social ethics. But what people have understood justice to involve has differed markedly over the centuries. Plato's utopian vision of the republic argues that justice requires the majority of citizens (to say nothing of women and slaves) to submit to the rule of philosophers, by formulating a particular interpretation of human nature. The prophetic oracles of Amos in the Jewish Scriptures insist that there is no justice in a society which allows the rich to impoverish and exploit the poor. The book of Deuteronomy encourages a community of brothers whose generosity to one another mirrors the generosity they have experienced from God. Contemporary democrats understand justice to involve a limited equality, a principle of equality in law and in the opportunity for all to vote in elections. The Pastorals present justice as a virtue for individuals within the believing community, but do not suggest that justice requires believing masters to free their slaves, not even in the seventh year (cf. Deut. 15), as we would do. Nor do the Pastorals share our sense that we owe opponents a just appreciation of their arguments. True to their Hellenistic context, the Pastorals are concerned to portray any different teaching in derogatory terms designed to prevent the reader from countenancing it, not to detail its particular strengths and weaknesses. Within the Bible, however, old formulations of what justice involves are not treated as sacrosanct. Rather the freedom to incorporate new insights into later versions is taken for granted. The biblical narratives, laws and exhortations assume that the struggle to gain both a fuller understanding of the implications of justice, and to express them in a more just society is the responsibility of each generation.

Alongside *justice, piety* is given a prominent place, as is usual in the Pastorals. *Faith* (REB *integrity*) and *love* are combined, as in I Cor. 13.2, 13, but, surprisingly, *hope* is not included here (cf. 1.1). *Endurance or fortitude* is the virtue which has replaced the Greek cardinal virtue *courage*, a virtue required in war. But the early followers of Jesus eschewed meeting violence with physical retaliation and so needed the virtue of *endurance* (e.g. Luke 8.15; Rom. 5.3–4; II Cor. 6.4; Col. 1.11; II Tim. 3.10; Titus 2.2). *Gentleness* is mentioned only here in the NT and is rare elsewhere in Greek literature. Timothy is exhorted to *struggle in the good contest of the faith* (REB interprets *the great race of faith*; cf. 4.10; I Cor. 9.25; II Tim. 4.7), an athletic metaphor replacing the earlier military metaphor in 1.18. Such a vision of life presents a stark alternative to love of money.

6.12   Timothy is also encouraged to *take hold of eternal life, to which you were called when you made the good confession before many witnesses. Eternal life* is usually conceived as a hope for the eschatological future, in the Pastorals (1.16; Titus 1.2; 3.7) as in Dan. 12.2. Here, it could refer to a quality of life, expressed by believers in the present, which would lead to eternal life at the eschaton. But it is more likely that *take hold of eternal life* is a metaphorical grasping at a reality which would become a possesion only at the eschaton. The reference to Timothy's good confession before many witnesses, since the verb is in the aorist tense, suggests a particular occasion when he made the confession. The only context mentioned in the epistle where such a confession would have been appropriate is at the council of elders' laying on of hands (4.14) but no confession is explicitly remarked there. Dibelius-Conzelmann propose baptism as the appropriate context, but the Pastorals never unambiguously refer to baptism (see the commentary on Titus 3.5). Either setting may be assumed but certainty is impossible. Timothy is urged to remain faithful to that confession *in the presence of God who gives life to all things* (cf. I Sam. 2.6; and, of Zeus, Diodorus Siculus 1.23). It is this belief that warrants the metaphor 'Father' for God (1.2).

6.13–16   The mention of Christ's presence leads into a reference to an incident in his historical life which is taken as exemplary: (the presence) *of Christ Jesus who bore witness with the good confession before Pontius Pilate* (REB paraphrases *who himself made that noble confession in his testimony before Pontius Pilate*). In the context of the Pastorals, this is a most surprising reference. Elsewhere in the NT, Pilate's full name occurs only in Luke 3.1; Acts 4.27, and Jesus' appearance before Pilate is mentioned nowhere else outside the Gospels. The content of his confession, unfortunately, is assumed, not detailed, and the result, crucifixion, is not specified. Never do the Pastorals mention crucifixion, not even in the context of references to the significance of his death (2.5–6; II Tim. 2.11–13; Titus 2.14). But does the exemplary significance of Jesus' confession before Pilate suggest that Timothy's past confession was also made before non–believers, and that he should still be ready to make such a confession? It is hard to decide, since I Tim. is concerned with the tasks Timothy is to perform within the believing community rather than outside it. The moderate and conservative lifestyle of believers is recommended so that outsiders would not be scandalised (3.7, 13; 5.2; 6.1), and only Paul is recognised as a missionary to Gentiles (2.7). Perhaps, then, the exemplary character of this incident in Jesus' life resides in his making the good confession, like Timothy, irrespective of the context in which it was made. On the other hand, II Tim. will encourage Timothy not to be ashamed of the testimony to the Lord, and will urge him and other believers to share in Paul's suffering for the faith (1.8; 2.3; 3.12). It is therefore not impossible that this reference to Jesus' confession before Pilate is intended to encourage Timothy's continuing fidelity in bearing testimony before unbelievers, even before governors. The concluding solemn injunction that Timothy should *keep the commandment unstained and blameless* (REB para-phrases *obey your orders without fault or favour)* seems to refer not just to the immediately preceding verses, but to the whole content of the epistle (cf. 6.20).

Until the appearing of our Lord Jesus Christ looks forward to the end of the struggle with Jesus' eschatological arrival. The language in which this expectation is expressed, his *appearing,* is characteristic of the Pastorals, and is used both of his eschatological appearance (II Tim. 4.1, 8; Titus 2.13) and of his historical appearance (II Tim. 1.10). The expression occurs only once in the NT outside the Pastorals, in II Thess. 2.8, where the Lord Jesus is expected to destroy the lawless one *by his appearing and his coming,* that is, at the eschaton. The language was used in Hellenistic literature of a god's or king's appearing to save people from illness or from war, and it carries regal overtones (see Dibelius-Conzelmann pp. 100–104). But I Tim. conceives Jesus' past appearing as saving people from ignorance and sin (1.12–17), and for eternal life at his future appearing (6.12, 17). Moreover, just as his past appearing is said to have happened at its own proper time (2.6), so his eschatological appearing is expected at its own proper time, since it will conform to God's purpose (REB paraphrases *God will bring about in his own good time).* The belief offers assurance of God's providential control. Praise of this God follows in terms reminiscent of 1.11 and 17: *blessed, only, whom no one has ever seen or can see.* But other distinctive terms, unparalleled in the NT, seem to be derived from the Jewish Scriptures in Greek: *Sovereign* (Ecclus 46.5; II Macc. 12.15); *King of kings* (III Macc. 5.35; cf. Dio Chrysostom 2.75), *Lord of lords* (Deut. 10.17; Ps. 136.3); *to him be honour and eternal dominion! Amen* (cf. I Peter 4.11; 5.11) reminds Timothy of whom he is to serve. Once again, we see the enrichment of Christian theological reflection from Hellenistic Judaism.

The wealthy

6.17–19

The last group about which the epistle gives advice to Timothy is the rich. The teaching is appropriately placed, after the positive affirmation of piety with self-sufficiency in a simple life (6.6–8), the warning against love of riches (6.5, 9–10), and the description of the kind of life Timothy should pursue until Christ's appearing, which encourages dedication to the Sovereign God (6.11–16). This eschatological perspective has led to the description of the wealthy as *the rich in the present age* (REB *rich in this world's goods*; cf. 4.8; II Tim. 4.10; Titus 2.12). In the light of this limitation, the wealthy are encouraged through Timothy *not to be proud*, a temptation for the rich because they were accorded loyalty and honour in the Graeco-Roman world, and *not to set their hope on such an uncertain thing as money but on God* (cf. 4.10; 5.5; Ps. 52.7; Prov. 8.10; 16.16). The description of God as one *who richly provides all things for us to enjoy* both acknowledges God as the source of material goods and discourages asceticism (cf. 4.3–4). Moreover, it forms the basis for the exhortation to do good, *being rich in good deeds*, specified as *giving generously* and *sharing*. In other words, rich members of the believing community are not to hoard or merely spend their wealth on conspicuous consumption, but, in recognition of God's generosity, to share with others, probably other believers. Not wealth itself but being rich in good deeds is approved. *Setting their hope on God* means that they should live in hope of Jesus' appearing (1.1; 6.14), and, hence, their present behaviour should seek God's approval rather than human honour. This eschatological perspective is particularly emphasised: *acquire treasure which will form a firm foundation for the future, so that they may grasp the life which is life indeed*. This *life which is life indeed* is more usually called *eternal life* (1.16; 6.12; Titus 1.2; 3.7) and, once, *the coming life* (4.8). The imagery is similar to that employed in Matt. 6.19–21 par, which contrasts earthly and heavenly treasure. The *firm or good foundation* is generosity and sharing. The social recognition which the wealthy in the Graeco-Roman world would normally have expected is replaced by concern for God's approval and the future eschatological life which he would give (see Kidd, 1990).

The final appeal and the grace

6.20–21

A concluding appeal to Timothy reinforces the previous exhortation, repeating some of the vocabulary of the introduction, to bring the epistle to a satisfying close. Timothy is to *guard the deposit* (REB *keep safe what has been entrusted to you*), that is, the teaching of the epistle, conceived as property which can be placed in a safe place, represented as Timothy himself. Commentators like Dibelius-Conzelmann, Houlden and Hanson contrast this image with the more dynamic understanding of faith in Romans, I and II Corinthians and Galatians. Again, this healthy teaching is contrasted with a summary of earlier statements about differerent teaching: *profane or irreligious chatter and contradictions of what is falsely called knowledge*. The reference to knowledge has prompted some commentators like Dibelius-Conzelmann to construe the different teaching as Gnostic (from the Greek word for knowledge), but *what is falsely called knowledge* is the antithesis of the epistle's positive teaching, conceived as *the knowledge of the truth* (2.4). Avoidance of such false teaching is encouraged by the assertion that *by laying claim to it some have missed the mark as regards*, or *strayed from, the faith* (cf. 1.6). Fidelity to the tradition, as set forth in the epistle's representation, is understood as fidelity to the faith, the Christian faith. Those of us who now read the epistle as part of a larger NT, however, and as part of long and various Christian traditions, can appreciate both its strengths and its shortcomings in this broader context.

Grace be with you (plural, cf. II Tim. 4.22) is a Christian adaptation of the normal closing good wishes of Hellenistic letters. There are, however, no exact NT parallels to the phraseology here and in II Tim. (cf. I Cor. 16.23; Gal. 6.18; Phil. 4.23, the closest examples). This includes the only occurence of the second person plural in the whole epistle. I Tim. 4.13 could, but need not, imply that the epistle was to be read to believers' assemblies at Ephesus. In any case, since the advice is clearly to be made known to other believers by Timothy, this final plural is appropriate (cf. Philemon 25).

Notes on 5.1–6.21

5.1 *Be harsh with* Literally, the Greek word means *strike at* and conveys the sense of a much more aggressive form of teaching than that advocated in 5.20, where Timothy is encouraged to rebuke or convict an elder who persists in sinning.

5.4 *Grandchildren* The Greek word can mean *descendants* in general, or, as here, more specifically *grandchildren*. This is the only occurence of the word in the NT, cf. Dio Chrysostom 21.21.

5.5 *Set her hope on God* cf. 4.10.

5.6 *As good as dead/ dead while living* The metaphor is also found in Philo, *Flight* 55.

The wife of one husband cf. 3.2,12 and Lightman and Zeisel, 1977.

5.10 *Saints* is a common designation of the faithful in Jewish as well as in Christian texts (Dan. 7.18; I Cor. 1.2; II Cor. 2.1).

5.13 *Gossips* only here in the NT, cf. Plutarch, *On listening to lectures* 3, *Mor.* 39A.

Busybodies only here in the NT, cf. Epictetus 3.1.21.

5.17 *Elders* Apart from the Pastorals, letters attributed to Paul never mention elders. The Jewish Scriptures assume that Jewish communities would be ruled by elders, e.g. Num. 11; 27.18-23; Deut. 34.9; II Macc. 13.13; 14.37. The NT also refers to Jewish elders (e.g. Matt. 26.3,57 and parr). Acts, like the Pastorals, refers to elders who rule Christian communities, e.g. Acts 11.30; 15.2. See also James 5.14; I Peter 5.1,5; II John 1; III John 1; and see Campbell, *Elders*, 1994.

5.21 *Angels who are chosen/elect angels* Nowhere else in the Bible are angels called elect. Elsewhere in the NT, the elect refers to Jesus (Luke 23.35; John 1.34; I Peter 2.4,6) or to believers (Matt. 24.22,24,31 and parr; Rom. 8.33; 16.13; Col. 3.12; II Tim. 2.10; Titus 1.1; I Peter 1.1; 2.9; II John 1,13; Rev 17.14).

Never prejudging the issue/without favour is a Hellenistic legal technical term, found only here in the NT and nowhere in the LXX.

Partiality is also found only here in the NT, never in the LXX, but often in Hellenistic literature, e.g. Polybius 5.51.8; 6.10.10; Diodorus Siculus 3.27.2. The related verb, however, is used in II Macc. 14.24 and Acts 5.36.

6.1-2 *Slaves* On slavery in the Graeco-Roman world, see M. I. Finley, *Ancient Slavery and Modern Ideology*, New York: Viking, 1980; T. Wiedemann, *Greek and Roman Slavery* London: Croom Helm, 1981; K. R. Bradley, *Slaves and Masters in the Roman Empire: A Study in Social Control*, New York: OUP, 1987.

6.1 *So that the name of God and the teaching are not brought into disrepute* echoes Isa. 52.5, quoted in Rom. 2.24.

6.4 Much of the vocabulary in this section is unique in relation to the rest of the NT, often it is also absent from the Septuagint, but it is found commonly in Hellenistic exhortation and Jewish Hellenistic writings. For details, see below.

Morbid enthusiasms occurs only here in the NT, cf. Plutarch, *Mor.* 546F.

Disputes about words cf. Titus 3.9, and nowhere else in the NT.
Base/evil suspicions occurs only here in the NT, cf. Ecclus 3.24; Josephus, *War* 1.277,631.

6.5 *Wrangles* is found only here in the NT, cf. Polybius 2.36.5.
Corrupted minds, in a moral sense, occurs only here in the NT, cf. Dio Chrysostom 26.10.
Dividends/a means of gain occurs only here and in the next verse in the NT, cf. Wisd. 14.2; Dio Chrysostom 32.9,20.

6.8 *Food* is found only here in the NT, cf. Epictetus *Enchiridion* 12.1.
Clothing occurs only here in the NT, cf. Aristotle, *Politics* 7.17.1336A; Philo, *The worse attacks the better* 19; Josephus, *War* 2.129.

6.9 *Harmful* is found only here in the NT, cf. Prov. 10.26; Xenophon, *Memorabilia* 1.3.11.

6.10 *Love of money* The noun occurs only here in the NT, but the adjective is found in II Tim. 3.2 in a description of people who would live in the last days; and in Luke 16.14 in a description of Jesus' opponents, cf. IV Macc. 1.26; Diog. L. 6.50. The vice would disqualify someone from becoming an overseer, 3.3.
Pierced occurs only here in the NT, cf. Diodorus Siculus 16.80; 19.84; Philo, *Against Flaccus* 1.

6.11 *Man of God* It is noteworthy that the word for *man* here means a human being.

6.16 *Unapproachable* is found only here in the NT, cf. Diodorus Siculus 1.32.1.

6.17 *Enjoyment* occurs only here and Heb. 11.25 in the NT, cf. III Macc. 7.16; Philo, *Moses* 2.70; Josephus, *Ant.* 2.52.

6.18 *Generous* is found only here in the NT, cf. Polybius 2.44.

6.19 *Acquire a treasure* occurs only here in the NT, cf. Epictetus 3.22.50, but a similar image is used in Matt. 6.19-22 parrs.
6.20 *The deposit/tradition* The Greek word used in the Pastorals (here and II Tim. 1.12,14) is different from that employed in other Paulines (e.g. I Cor. 11.2; Gal. 1.14).
Avoid/turn away from cf. 1.6.
Profane cf. 4.7.
Chatter cf. II Tim. 2.16, but nowhere else in the NT, cf. Epictetus 2.17.8.
Contradictions occurs only here in the NT, cf. Plutarch, *The principle of cold* 17, *Mor.* 953B.
Falsely called occurs only here in the NT, cf. Plutarch, *On brotherly love* 4, *Mor.* 479E; Philo, *Moses* 2.171.
Knowledge cf. I Cor 8.1,7,11.

6.21 *Missed the mark* cf. 1.6.

II TIMOTHY

Outline

The opening chapter contrasts Paul's faithful acceptance of his suffering for the faith with the behaviour of his Asian associates who had deserted him, and encourages Timothy's continuing loyalty by recounting Onesiphorus' visit to Paul in prison. The main body of the letter invites Timothy to share in suffering by following the examples of Paul and Christ Jesus, and tries to persuade him to avoid the passion for controversy indulged by false teachers. Rather, he is encouraged to set an example by his faithful pursuit of theological virtues and by his gentle correction of others' faults, in a context in which he is warned about the future vicious behaviour of believers in the last times. Again, Paul's example is to inspire Timothy and all believers to endure persecution. Timothy is to continue following the teachings of the Jewish Scriptures, in the expectation of a future eschatological judgment, and the reward for suffering which this would bring. The appeal for Timothy's loyalty is made more urgent by the prospect of Paul's imminent martyrdom.

The opening and introduction to the epistle: contrasting portraits
1.1–18

1.1 The epistle reflects on the significance and effects of Paul's imprisonment and his sufferings for the good news, but the opening description of him as *apostle of Christ Jesus* (cf. I Tim. 1.1) *by the will of God* (cf. II Cor. 1.1; Eph. 1.1; Col. 1.1) highlights his status within the believing community and justifies his writing to Timothy. Moreover, the reference to God's *promise of life, fulfilled in Christ Jesus* (cf. I Tim. 1.14) sets the sufferings in a larger theological context, and it will gradually become clear that *life* refers not just to present mortal existence but also to immortality beyond death (1.10; 2.8, 11–13; 4.6–8, 18). As in the case of I Tim., the exhortation is framed by references to the hope of future eschatological eternal life (1.1; 4.1–8, 18). Hence present suffering, terrible though it is seen to be, is understood from the perspective of eternity.

1.2 Timothy is addressed as *dear son/beloved child* (cf. I Cor. 4.17). I Tim. had called him Paul's legitimate child to distinguish him from others who were giving different teaching, but this metaphorical address strikes a much warmer, more intimate note. Again, as in I Tim. 1.2, the usual Pauline greeting, *grace and peace*, is expanded to include *mercy*, and the Lord's mercy will be requested in 1.16, 18 (see also 4.16). God is called, metaphorically, *Father*, and Christ Jesus is recognised as *our Lord*, as in I Tim. 1.2.

1.3–5 The thanksgiving refers to God as *the God of my forefathers*, an expression which emphasises the continuity of service to God performed both by Paul and by his ancestors. Judaism, then, is seen in a positive light, and, surprisingly, no reference is made to Paul's former life as a persecutor of believers (contrast I Tim. 1.12–16). A similar appreciation of Timothy's fidelity to the faith of his family will be expressed in verse 5, and Timothy's familiarity with the Jewish Scriptures from early childhood will be commended in 3.15. This kind of family loyalty is frequently praised in Hellenistic inscriptions. Moreover, these references evince the importance of family nurture in the faith, which was to be ensured by the exemplary heads of households depicted in I Tim. 3.4, 12 (and see Titus 1.6). And Paul's service of this God is defined as service *with a clear* or *pure conscience*, free from any sense of wrong-doing. Futhermore, the affectionate tone of the address to Timothy is developed by specifying that he is included in Paul's *prayers, night and day* (cf. I Tim. 5.5 of the real widow). As in I Tim., prayer is understood as essential for the fulfilment of God's purpose, and Paul provides an example for imitation (see I Tim. 2.1–3). That Timothy's affection for Paul equals his for Timothy is intimated by the reference to Timothy's *tears*, presumably when they parted. This naturally leads to the mention of Paul's *longing to see* him, with the expectation of a joyful reunion. The tender relationship between an older apostle and his younger delegate allows an expression of confidence in Timothy's *sincere faith*, while mentioning the faith of his *grandmother* and *mother* encourages his continuing fidelity, a major theme of the whole epistle (1.13–14; chapter 2; 3.10–17; 4.1–5).

1.6–10 Timothy's *sincere faith* then becomes the reason for Paul's reminder that Timothy should *stir into flame God's gift* or *charisma*, a gift associated with Paul's laying on of hands. In I Tim. 4.14, Timothy's charisma had been associated with the council of elders' laying on of hands, and the difference reflects the distinctive interests of each passage. I Tim. is concerned about Timothy's relations with the local leadership, whereas II Tim. focuses on Timothy's closeness to Paul. Moreover, the spirit which Timothy is understood to have received from God is defined both negatively, *no cowardly spirit*, and positively, a spirit *of power, love and self-discipline*. It is this spirit and the power it brings that inspires fidelity even in the face of the persecution and suffering that Timothy is encouraged to share. It is not, however, a spirit which engenders violent retaliation. The verse makes clear that only God is truly powerful, and only God's spirit can ensure the continuing loyalty of Timothy, with the *love* and *good judgment* required. On this foundation, Timothy is urged not to be *ashamed of the testimony to our Lord*. Why there should be any question of his being ashamed is immediately made clear. Timothy is to be ashamed neither of the testimony nor of Paul himself as the Lord's *prisoner* (cf. Phil. 1.7, 12–14, an epistle with many resemblances to II Tim. REB paraphrases *imprisoned for his sake*). Paul is writing from prison, and he can be called the Lord's prisoner because he is imprisoned on account of his preaching the good news. If Timothy is to be loyal to the good news, he should not be ashamed of its testimony nor of the person who has been preaching it. Phil. 1.13 provides a similar reason for Paul's imprisonment. As a leading missionary, Paul was more likely to come to the authorities' attention than were other, less prominent believers, but his associates might naturally come under suspicion too. So Timothy is encouraged to accept his *share of suffering through the power that comes from God* (cf. 1.7). Reminding him that it is God who saved them both, not for *any merit* of theirs, but *for his own purpose and of his own grace,* calls on Timothy's own experience to justify his reliance on God's power in any future trials. The present existence of believers is conceived as salvation, already granted by God, but also awaiting completion at the eschaton (4.1, 8). And because God is eternal, God's purpose is eternal, *from all eternity* (cf. I Tim. 6.17). Moreover, this passage explains that God's eternal purpose and his grace, given to those who live *in Christ Jesus,* had been made known by the appearing of Christ Jesus, who is therefore appropriately recognised as *Saviour.* He is said to have *broken the power of death and brought life and immortality to light,* presumably at his resurrection from the dead (2.8, 11). The confession, therefore, does not imply that all believers would escape death. On the contrary, Paul is expecting imminent martyrdom (4.6–8). Rather, Christ's resurrection is understood to guarantee the resurrection of faithful believers at the eschatological judgment (2.11–13; 4.1, 8). This assurance of life after death serves to encourage present fidelity in a context of persecution for the faith.

1.11–12 A description of Paul's behaviour now creates an example for Timothy to follow. Paul is presented as herald and apostle, but also as teacher, like Timothy, and this is the reason for his suffering. Nevertheless, he is *not ashamed.* Moreover, the cause of his lack of shame, in spite of his socially disgraceful circumstances as a prisoner, is explained: *because I know whom I have trusted,* that is, the God who saves through Christ Jesus. Hence, Paul can express confidence that God would *keep safe what he put into my charge until that day,* the eschatological day of judgment (4.1). In other words, God would guard the teaching which makes his purpose known, and which the epistle tries to encapsulate, until the eschaton. This conception of the teaching as a deposit, entrusted to Paul and passed on to Timothy, to be passed on to other people (2.2), is essentially conservative. It shares with Hellenistic philosophical writings a concern to preserve the true tradition against corruptions, and contrasts with the greater openness, dynamism, and confidence in the believing communities expressed in other Paulines. There is a certain irony in presenting the epistle's teaching in this way, as a physical deposit, since the Pastorals develop the Pauline tradition in new ways, highlighting the dialectic between present and eschatological salvation, and enriching its ethical and theological conceptions from Jewish Hellenistic and pagan philosophical traditions. Nevertheless, Paul is presented as a person who passes on his last testament to his younger associate.

1.13–14 The successful transmission of the teaching, however, depends on Timothy's response, or rather, depends on Timothy's acceptance of God's empowerment. So Timothy is exhorted to follow Paul's example by *holding to the outline of sound* or *healthy teaching* which he received from Paul. Now this teaching is understood to be prototypical. In I Tim. 1.16, the change brought about in Paul's life by the mercy of Christ Jesus was presented as prototypical. Here, the teaching is what makes God's saving purpose known, and that purpose is to bring a new life, a life characterised *by the faith and the love* (cf. I Tim. 1.14) which are *in Christ Jesus*. And, as God had been said to safeguard the deposit entrusted to Paul, so Timothy is also to *keep the treasure* with the help of the Holy Spirit. This Holy Spirit is described as dwelling in *us*, and *us*, in the context, means Paul and Timothy, but Titus 3.5 suggests that the Holy Spirit would inspire all believers. The whole passage emphasises that only God's inspiration can ensure human fidelity in the face of suffering and death.

1.15–18 Further encouragement is offered to Timothy through examples of disloyalty and loyalty from other associates of Paul. The reader is expected to recoil in horror from the reminder that *everyone in Asia* had deserted Paul. The rhetorical exaggeration, which will shortly be modified by reference to the Asian believer Onesiphorus, increases the effect. Fidelity to Paul is required because he is suffering not as a private individual but as the representative apostle, through whom others received the good news, and whose exemplary heroism should foster imitation. *Asia* was a Roman province in modern western Turkey, which included Ephesus as its capital, and Timothy is understood still to be there (1.18; 4.12, 19; I Tim. 1.3). Among the deserters, *Phygelus and Hermogenes* are named, and their names balance those of the two faithful exemplars for Timothy, Paul and Onesiphorus. They are mentioned only here in the NT. *Onesiphorus* is also unknown outside this epistle but he is represented as an Ephesian to whose household greetings are sent (4.19), and as a worthy model for Timothy in his refusal to be ashamed of Paul's chains (REB paraphrases *a prisoner*). Moreover, his hastening to Rome in order to find Paul and minister to his needs is just what the epistle encourages Timothy to do (4.9, 21). *Rome*, then, is the place of Paul's imprisonment. Paul's gratitude to Onesiphorus is expressed in his request both that the Lord grant him mercy, and that the Lord grant his household mercy, apparently in recognition of his family's supporting role. This introduction to the epistle, which recalls the past and sets the scene for the following exhortation, is concluded by reminding Timothy that he is well aware of Onesiphorus' past service at Ephesus, the temporary place of Timothy's residence. No less is required of Timothy by the instructions in chapters 2–4.

Notes on 1.1–18

1.3 *I give thanks* Again, as in I Tim. 1.12, the Greek expression is different from that normally used in the Paulines.
Forefathers occurs only here in the NT, but frequently in Hellenistic inscriptions.
Clean or *pure conscience* see the note on I Tim. 1.5.
1.4 *Tears* cf. the mention of Paul's tears in II Cor. 2.4; Acts 20.19, and the weeping of the Ephesian elders, Acts 20.37.
Longing to see cf. Rom. 1.11; I Thess. 3.6.
Make my happiness or joy complete cf. Phil. 2.2.
1.5 *The sincerity of your faith*, literally, *sincere faith*, the same expression as that in I Tim. 1.5.
Mother Acts 16.1 describes Timothy's mother as a Jewish Christian but does not name her, nor is Timothy's grandmother mentioned. Indeed, the Greek word for grandmother appears only here in the NT. Another grandmother and mother are mentioned together and named in Plutarch, *Agis* 4.1, suggesting that such references would not have seemed unusual in Hellenistic literature. Acts pictures Timothy's father

as an unbelieving pagan, but I and II Tim. emphasise that Paul is his spiritual father.

1.6 *Stir into flame* occurs only here in the NT; cf. Plutarch, *Pericles* 1.4.

1.7 *No cowardly spirit* is literally *not a spirit of cowardice*. The expression occurs only here in the NT, but a similar understanding is expressed in different words in Rom. 8.15.

Self-discipline or *good judgment* is found only here in the NT, with the related verb in Titus 2.4. It is reckoned a cardinal virtue in Greek philosophy, cf. Plutarch, *Table talk* 3.6.1 and 7.8.4, *Mor.* 653C and 713C, and is integrated into the theological ethics of II Tim. by representing it as a gift from God.

1.9 *Called us to a dedicated life* is literally *called us with a holy calling* cf. I Thess. 4.7.

Brought salvation/saved in the past tense. According to the Pastorals, Christ's past appearing brought salvation to believers, although his eschatological appearing would complete the gift with eternal life. This is why both God and Christ are called Saviour (I Tim. 1.1; 2.3; 4.10; II Tim. 1.8–10; Titus 1.3–4; 2.11, 13; 3.4, 6). This view is distinctive among the letters attributed to Paul. In other Paulines, salvation or being saved is presented as a hope for the future (e.g. Rom. 1.16; 13.11; I Thess. 5.8–9). Only Rom. 8.24 comes near to the Pastorals' view.

Any merit is literally *according to our works*. The phrase used in Romans is 'works of the law', which are contrasted with faith.

Called for God's purpose cf. Rom. 8.28.

1.10 *Broken the power of death* is literally *abolished death*. I Cor. 15.26 pictures Christ's defeat of death as a future eschatological event, but this passage seems to represent Jesus' resurrection as accomplishing that defeat. Nevertheless, II Tim., like I Cor., expects believers who die to be resurrected only at the eschaton (4.1, 8).

1.11 *Herald, apostle, teacher* cf. I Tim. 2.7. I Cor. 12.28 separates apostles and teachers.

1.12 *What is put into my charge* is literally *the deposit*, an expression found in the Pastorals but not in other Paulines, cf. 1.4 and I Tim. 6.20.

1.14 *Guard the treasure* is literally *guard the good deposit*, cf. above.

Holy Spirit is mentioned only here and in Titus 3.5 in the Pastorals, but the spirit, without further definition, occurs in 1.7; I Tim. 4.1.

1.15 *Asia* is named elsewhere in the Paulines: Rom. 16.5; I Cor. 16.19; II Cor. 1.8, but it is impossible to fit the geographical and personal references of the Pastorals into any reconstruction of Paul's ministry during the period reflected in other Paulines or in Acts. See, for example, Kelly, 1963, pp 6–10.

Relieved or *refreshed* occurs only here and Rom. 15.32 in the NT.

1.16 *A prisoner* is literally *my chains*. The reference assumes that Paul is not only imprisoned but also chained in a manner which would add to his sufferings, cf. Eph. 6.20, the only other reference to chains in epistles attributed to Paul. The same contrast between those who remained faithful to Paul and those who did not, however, is made in Phil. 1.15–19.

Timothy is encouraged to share in suffering, following the examples of Paul and Jesus Christ
2.1–13

2.1–2   The repeated address to Timothy as *my son* or *child* (cf. 1.2) reminds him of his dependence upon Paul and of the common expectation that he should be like his spiritual father. He is urged once more to *take strength from the grace (of God) which is ours in Christ Jesus,* a summary of the exhortation in 1.6–10 which assures him that God's inspiration can give him the strength for his task. The first part of that task is to pass on to other faithful people what he had heard from Paul before *many witnesses* in order that they may teach others. This concern for the reliable transmission of correct teaching was shared with Hellenistic philosophical literature. *In the presence of many witnesses* is a possible translation of the Greek which suggests that others would recognise whether Timothy was faithfully repeating Paul's teaching or not. The phrase could also be translated *through many witnesses,* suggesting that Timothy had heard Paul's teaching both directly from him and through others. The passage creates the impression that the teaching is to be accepted without question and passed on without alteration. But it immediately becomes clear that the reader is not merely to be passive. Rather, he is to be actively engaged in putting the teaching into practice, by faithfully transmitting teaching which has led to Paul's chained imprisonment.

2.3–7   So, the earlier appeal to Timothy is repeated: he is to share in suffering (1.8). His teaching role and his loyalty to Paul would involve hardship like that of a soldier or a competing athlete or a working farmer. Each of the images highlights a different perspective on Timothy's work. A soldier should not be *involved in the affairs of everyday life if he is to give satisfaction to his commanding officer.* Hence Timothy is to express the same dedication in order to give satisfaction to Paul. That *no athlete wins a prize unless he abides by the rules* encourages Timothy to abide by the rules of the faith which would bring him the prize of eternal life (1.10). That *the farmer who does the work has first claim on the crop* assures him that his task is essential and that his reward is certain. Timothy is urged to ponder these perspectives, but understanding is not conceived as the fruit of reflection, as it was in Hellenistic philosophical exhortation, but as the gift of the Lord.

2.8–10   Moreover, Timothy's reflections are to include his remembrance of Jesus' resurrection and Messianic status. Remembering that Jesus had been raised from the dead would help Timothy to look beyond suffering and even death to God's vindication. *Born of David's line* (cf. Rom. 1.3) draws attention to Jesus' royal authority which requires Timothy's service. Both statements also emphasise Jesus' humanity which Timothy shares. The confession is presented as the central Christian belief, as Paul's good news, for which he is *exposed to hardship,* the kind of hardship that Timothy is to share (2.3). So Paul's experience is described as exemplary. He is even *fettered like a criminal* (cf. Philemon 13), but he rejects any suggestion that he is a criminal (4.6–8, 17–18), and the image of being chained is used to point up the limited effectiveness of such a physical bond: *but the word of God is not fettered,* as is demonstrated by the epistle (cf. Phil. 1.12–14). Moreover, Paul's endurance is understood to be *for the sake of the chosen ones,* so that *they may attain the glorious and eternal salvation which is in Christ Jesus.* Here, the completion of present salvation with the reward of eternal life at the eschaton is seen as the hope of all faithful believers, who are called *chosen ones* because their salvation depends ultimately on God's gift (1.9–10). Their attainment of this reward gives purpose to Paul's endurance. His imprisonment is not perceived as a personal matter, but as the effect of his preaching the good news (1.11–12) and as a test of his fidelity to those beliefs. Any failure on his part, therefore, would affect not only his own future but also that of other believers. As the Pastorals repeatedly stress, belief is to be expressed in practice.

2.11–13   What living *in Christ Jesus* means is then explained. The statement is introduced with the reassurance: *here is a saying you may trust,* both to highlight its importance and to encourage its acceptance. The balanced rhythm of the statement has suggested to commentators that this is an extract from a liturgical confession. Unfortunately, we have no independent evidence which would allow us to verify the suggestion. In any case, the content of the confession, with its focus on Christ's endurance and fidelity, is exactly what is required to ground the epistle's argument. Paul's example of endurance is shown to conform to Christ's, and Timothy is to follow both examples if he is to continue to live *in Christ Jesus. Died with him,* in the past tense, is a metaphor for dying to an old lifestyle, as in Rom. 6.3, but the new way of life may also require martyrdom (4.6). *We shall live with him* looks forward to eternal life at the eschaton (4.8, cf. Rom. 6.8). *If we endure* recalls the earlier description of Paul's endurance in 2.10. *We shall reign with him* conceives eternal life in regal terms. The image of a crown had been used in 2.5, and would be used again in 4.8. But the Pastorals contain no suggestion that believers would join Christ Jesus in judging the living and the dead (4.1; cf. I Cor. 6.2; Matt. 19.28 par). This positive expectation, which echoes other Pauline passages, however, is followed by a warning. *If we deny him, he will deny us* finds no parallel in other Pauline epistles, but a similar warning occurs in Matt. 10.33 par. Later in the epistle, unfaithful believers during the last days are expected to deny the power of piety (3.5, cf. Titus 1.16). The warning serves to emphasise the importance of present endurance. *If we are faithless* represents another possibility which the epistle seeks to counter, but this time assurance is offered: *he remains faithful, for he cannot deny himself.* The whole of Jesus' life is conceived in terms of his fidelity in order to encourage Timothy's fidelity and the fidelity of those he would teach. Timothy has been shown three examples of loyalty in the face of hardship, those of Onesiphorus, Paul and Christ Jesus. Since Timothy is to live *in Christ Jesus,* his life is to conform to Jesus', as Paul's is seen to do.

Notes on 2.1–13

2.1 *Take strength from the grace* REB adds *God's.* Compare Rom. 4.10: *strong in faith;* Eph. 6.10 *strong in the Lord.* Whereas Romans and Galatians contrast works of the law and faith, the Pastorals contrast works in general and grace.

2.3–4 The image of a *soldier* is also used in I Cor. 9.7; II Cor. 10.3; Phil. 2.25. *Not involved in the affairs of everyday life* is a prerequisite of philosophical reflection, according to Hellenistic writings like Epictetus 3.22.69, where the same phrase occurs. It is found nowhere else in the NT. *His commanding officer* is literally *the one who enrolled him*, and is also unique in the NT, cf. Diodorus Siculus 12.67.

2.5 The image of a *competing athlete* is also used in I Cor. 9.24–27, where, however, it is developed differently. The same image underlies Paul's claim in 4.7 that he had run the race. *Wins a prize* is literally *crowned.* Compare the expectation that Paul would receive a crown of righteousness in 4.8.

The crop The same image is used in I Cor. 9.7, 10, but in relation to the support of apostles. Here it refers to eschatological reward.

2.8 *My gospel* or *good news* cf. Rom. 2.16; 16.25. Here the reference emphasises the distinction between the authentic Pauline teaching which the epistle claims to represent and alternative teaching which will be mentioned in 2.16–18.

2.9 *Exposed to hardship* The verb is used only here and 4.5 in the NT, cf. Polybius 3.72.5. In 2.3, the same verb is used with the prefix *with* to mean *share in suffering or take your share of hardship.*

2.10 *Chosen ones* The Jewish Scriptures describe the members of the covenant community as God's chosen ones, e.g. I Chron. 16.13; Ps. 89.3. Some NT writings take over this description for Christians, cf. Titus 1.1; Rom. 8.33; Col. 3.12; I Peter 1.1.

Glorious and eternal salvation is literally *salvation with eternal glory* cf. II Cor. 4.17.

The good and the bad teacher
2.14–26

2.14–15   Timothy is exhorted to *keep on reminding people* about Paul's and Jesus' endurance, and to charge people *not to dispute about words*. *Before God* reminds the reader of the awesome responsibility of teaching (cf. I Tim. 5.21). Disputing about words is characterised as harmful in itself, but, in addition, it is said to *ruin those who listen*. A contrast is made with the wholesome effects of Paul's teaching, responding to which would bring eternal life (1.10; 2.10). Moreover, Timothy is exhorted to become an exemplary teacher too, by showing himself to be a person whom *God approves*. The desire merely to impress human beings is to be replaced by concern with God's approval. Later, in 4.3, the fear is expressed that in the future people would tolerate only those teachers who would pander to their own likings. Timothy, on the contrary, is to be *a worker with no cause for shame*. The argument suggests that, by behaving as someone who is not ashamed of Paul's teaching, which has brought him sufferings in prison, Timothy would have no reason to be ashamed himself (1.8, 12, 15). REB's *keep strictly to the true gospel* is a paraphrase of *cut a straight path for the statement of the truth*. *The statement of the truth* is an evaluation of the good news, used also in I Tim. 6.5 (cf. Eph. 1.13), which understands it as the truth about God's purpose for all people.

2.16–18   The behaviour advocated for Timothy is immediately contrasted with its opposite: *profane empty chatter* (cf. I Tim. 6.20; REB *empty and irreligious chatter)*, which Timothy is warned to avoid because of its effects in leading people into even more impiety. The Pastorals see *piety* as fundamental for believers' well-being (see 3.5; I Tim. 3.16; 4.7–8; 6.3, 5–6, 11). It serves to intimate their need to acknowledge their dependence on God's grace. The medical metaphor used in calling Pauline teaching *healthy* or *sound* is developed to describe opposing teaching as diseased, and the particular expression, *spreading like gangrene*, picks up the earlier suggestion that impiety would lead to even more impiety. The same image of gangrene is used in Plutarch, *How to tell a flatterer* 24, *Mor.* 65D. Naming opposing teachers particularises the negative portrait, and providing two names corresponds to the two named faithful exemplars, Paul and Christ Jesus (2.8–13). *Philetus* is mentioned nowhere else in the NT, but *Hymenaeus* had been named in I Tim. 1.20, along with Alexander, as people whom Paul had delivered to Satan so that they would learn not to slander. The hope of their reform, suggested by that passage, is now understood to have been vain in the case of Hymenaeus (and see 4.14 on Alexander, if the reference is to the same character). Up to this point, and again in verse 23, opposing teachings are described with the conventional negative epithets of Hellenistic philosophical exhortation (see I Tim. 1.3–6; 6.3–5, 20–21). But now, the content of some of the teaching is specified: *saying that our resurrection has already taken place*. This is probably the correct interpretation of: *saying resurrection has happened already*. In the confession of 2.11, *we shall live with him* is presented as a future eschatological expectation, as in Rom. 6.8. This opposing teaching, however, seems to be using resurrection language metaphorically to capture the sense of their new life in Christ. Eph. 2.6 and Col. 2.12; 3.1 also use resurrection language metaphorically in the same way. Why is objection taken to this form of expression here? The Pastorals insist that the present life of believers be understood as salvation, but they also teach that salvation would only reach fruition at the eschaton with God's gift of eternal life. II Tim. 4.1 and 8, moreover, emphasise the expectation of eschatological judgment. Perhaps, then, objection is taken to the metaphorical use of resurrection language because it might encourage people to suppose that their future eternal life is already guaranteed, irrespective of how they behave. II Tim. stresses, on the contrary, that only those who remain loyal both to Paul himself and to his teaching could expect the reward of eternal life at the eschatological judgment (4.1, 6–8, 18). This is why Philetus and Hymenaeus are said to be *wide of the truth* and to be *undermining people's faith*. Their teaching, however, is not formally refuted with counter-arguments. The earlier appeal to a sure saying, which expresses the alternative view (2.11–13), and a further appeal to God's judgment, are presented as sufficient warning against what is described as a corrupt and corrupting falsehood.

2.19–21 The striking image of *God's foundation stone*, which *stands firm*, and which bears the *inscription or seal*, highlights the continuing relevance of an old message. *The Lord knows his own* echoes Num. 16.5. The context tells the story of the revolt of Korah and his followers against Moses, and of God's destruction of them. A reference to the same incident is also used as a warning in Jude 11. Hymenaeus, Philetus and their followers are understood as rebellious people whom God would distinguish from *his own* in the believing community, as God had distinguished and destroyed Korah and his companions. Moreover, in 3.17, Timothy will be encouraged to behave as a *man of God*, a description of Moses in Deut. 33.1. The warning, however, is followed by another allusion to the Jewish Scriptures, this time to a combination of Isa. 26.13 and Ps. 6.8, which urges repentance: *everyone who takes the Lord's name upon his lips must forsake wickedness. Wickedness* or *injustice* is the opposite of the *justice* which Timothy is to pursue (verse 22), and describes the false teaching which is said to bring people to ruin.

Repentance is further encouraged through the figure of household utensils, which represent different kinds of people. Those that are *valued* or *honoured* represent those who are faithful to the teaching and who have forsaken wickedness, while those that are *cheap* or *dishonoured* represent those who offer different teaching. The figure is not fully sustained, however, because cleansing would not change a wooden vessel into a golden one, whereas cleansing in the sense of forsaking injustice would change an opponent into an honoured and sanctified member of the believing community, *useful to the master of the house*, God. Then that person would be *ready for every good work* (REB paraphrases *fit for an honourable purpose*). By referring to *every good work*, this reference reinforces other teaching that belief should find expression in good works (3.17; 4.5). Once again, as in I Tim. 3.15, the church is understood as God's household.

2.22–26 After this negative portrait of false teachers, Timothy is exhorted to express contrary tendencies. He is to *flee youthful passions* (REB paraphrases *turn away from wayward passions*). That Timothy is young (cf. I Tim. 4.12) is assumed, as is also the common Hellenistic view that the young would be plagued by passions unless they mastered them. The metaphor of *fleeing* the passions balances the metaphor of *pursuing* the virtues. These virtues are then listed. *Justice,* a cardinal virtue among the ancient Greeks, is integrated into the christological beliefs of the epistle by representing the Lord as the just judge (4.8). REB's *integrity* interprets *faith*, in the sense of *fidelity*. In common with the other Pastorals and with Paul in I Cor. 13, *love* is considered centrally important, and, as here, faith and love are linked in I Cor. 13.13. *Peace* contrasts with the upset caused by the false teachers (2.18). The opening salutation sees *peace* as God's gift in Christ Jesus. This peace, however, is not reckoned to exclude suffering (3.12). Timothy is further encouraged in his pursuit of the virtues by associating him with *all who call upon the Lord from a pure heart* (cf. I Tim. 1.5; REB paraphrases *all who worship the Lord in singleness of mind*). In case the contrast with false teachers had been forgotten, their teaching is briefly recalled as *foolish and wild speculations that breed quarrels*. Now Timothy can be reminded that he is *a servant of the Lord*, who should not be *quarrelsome or aggressive*, but *kindly to all*. What this involves is then explained: a *good teacher* is to *bear evil without resentment* (REB's *tolerant* is too weak to capture the sense of the Greek), and to *discipline those who oppose* him with *gentleness* or *humility*. In the Graeco-Roman world, there were Cynic philosophers who adopted an aggressive mode of teaching, haranguing their audience in order to shock them into adopting a preferred lifestyle, not unlike the manner of some US chat-show hosts. But most Hellenistic philosophical literature favours kindly reproval as this epistle does. This gentle discipline is encouraged in the expectation that God would grant the opponents *repentance*, which REB interprets as *a change of heart*, so that they would come to a *recognition of the truth*. This recognition is not only an intellectual assent, but also involves a different way of life. The change is pictured both as a *sobering up* or *return to their senses*, and as an escape from *the slanderer's snare*, probably *the devil's snare*, caught in which they had become the devil's agents instead of God's, living aggressively uncontrolled lives. This portrait of bad teachers is designed to cause repugnance in the reader and, in that way, to promote conformity to the portrait of the good teacher, as in Hellenistic writings.

Notes on 2.14–26

2.15 *Show yourself worthy of God's approval* is literally *present yourself to God as one approved*   cf. Rom. 12.1; 16.10.
A worker The noun is used with the adjectives *deceitful* and *evil* in II Cor. 11.13; Phil. 3.2, of those whom Paul opposes.

Cut a straight path The metaphor occurs only here in the NT, and only in Prov. 3.6; 11.5 in the Jewish Scriptures.

2.19 The Greek particle translated *but* is not used in other Paulines, and the adjective *firm* is found only here in the NT. *Foundation*, however, occurs in Rom. 15.20; I Cor. 3.10–12, as well as in I Tim. 6.19.

2.20 *Utensils* for people is a figure also used in Rom. 9.21, although there it is developed differently.

2.21 *Master* The Greek word occurs only in the Pastorals among the epistles attributed to Paul, cf. I Tim. 6.1–2; Tit 2.9 of the master of slaves. The word was commonly used to refer to God in Greek literature (e.g. Plato, *Euthydemus* 302D) and was taken over by Hellenistic Jewish writers (e.g. Josephus, *Ant.* 8.111).

2.22 *All who worship the Lord* Some manuscripts omit *all*.

2.23 *Wild* is literally *uninstructed* or *uneducated*. This is the only instance of its use in the NT, but it was commonly employed to caricature opponents in Hellenistic writings (e.g. Josephus, *Ant.* 2.285).

2.24 *Kindly* The adjective is used to describe Paul's demeanour in I Thess. 2.7, and to describe Moses' in Philo, *Moses* 1.72.
Bear evil without resentment is found only here in the NT, but is advocated in Hellenistic literature (e.g. Wisd. 2.19; Josephus, *War* 1.624).

2.26 *Sober up* The verb occurs only here in the NT, but the metaphor was commonly used to suggest a change to a more moderate lifestyle in Hellenistic literature (e.g. Dio Chrysostom 4.77; Philo, *Allegorical Interpretation* 2.60; Josephus, *Ant.* 6.241).
Escape from the devil's snare in which they have been trapped and held at his will The personal pronouns in this clause leave it open to more than one translation. REB's rendering seems the most likely, but it could also mean *escape from the devil's snare, being captured by God's servant to do his will* or *escape from the devil's snare, after being captured by him, to do God's will*.

The character of people in the last days
3.1–9

3.1–7 Timothy's fidelity to Paul and the teaching, and his setting a present good example for others to follow, is further encouraged by a vision of worse to come. As in I Tim. 4.1–3, general Jewish apocalyptic expectations of distress in the last days before the eschaton are moulded to focus on impiety which is understood to lead to unethical behaviour. REB's *remember the final age of this world is to be a time of turmoil* paraphrases *and know this, that in the last days there will come times of stress*. A long list of vicious personal characteristics, made memorable by the assonance and alliteration of the Greek, describes the kind of people who would flourish then. This character sketch represents what most people in the ancient Graeco-Roman world and today would find abhorrent. Such people would be devoid of the virtues advocated by the epistle and would love the wrong objects, self and money, instead of God. They would be arrogant boasters and aggressive fools (see the notes for details). Their dispositions are contrary to those recommended to Timothy in 2.22–26. They would cloak their pleasure-loving in a hypocritical piety which neither recognises God's power nor lives from God's inspiration (cf. 1.7–8). Timothy is required to *keep clear* of people with these characteristics. Since this command is expressed in the present tense, and the verbs in verses 6–7 are also in the present, in contrast to the verbs in verses 1–5, which are in the future tense, does this suggest that the epistle envisages such people as already making an appearance, and in that way pictures the present as already part of the last days? This seems unlikely. Rather the present tense is best understood as gnomic. Verses 6–7 describe what such people habitually do, and Timothy, and those to whom he passes the teaching (2.2), are therefore encouraged to avoid them whenever they appear. That they would *insinuate themselves into private houses* and attract only *silly women, incapable of attaining to a knowledge of the truth* draws on common prejudices against women to convince the reader that these people would gain a following only among the foolish. Moreover, Graeco-Roman men would have been appalled at the prospect of their women coming under the influence of other men, and at the disruption of their households this would cause.

3.8–9 These vicious people are pictured as analogous to *Jannes and Jambres* (cf. 2.19). According to Ex. 7.11 and 8.18–19, Egyptian magicians opposed Moses, and later Jewish legends supplied their names, as here (cf. CD 5.17–19; Testament of Solomon 25.3–4). This again suggests the influence of Hellenistic Jewish traditions on the Pastorals. As usual, two names are given (cf. 2.17). Like Moses, Timothy will be called a *man of God* in 3.17 (cf. Deut. 33.1). That even these people's *successes will be short-lived,* like those of the Egyptian magicians, implies also that the success of wicked people already present in the community (2.17; 3.13) would be equally limited. The assurance justifies Timothy's avoidance of such people.

Notes on 3.1–9

3.1 *The last days* cf. Acts 2.17; James 5.3; II Peter 3.3; Jude 18. This particular expression is not used in other Paulines.
Times of stress/turmoil In the NT, the adjective is used only here to describe the last days. In Matt. 8.28 it describes the two demoniacs. In Greek literature it mostly describes fierce animals. Josephus, *Ant.* 4.1, uses it, however, to describe the hard life of the Hebrews in the wilderness.
3.2 *Love nothing but self and money* is literally *people will be lovers of self and lovers of money. Lovers of self* occurs only here in the NT, but was commonly deplored in Hellenistic and Jewish Hellenistic writings (e.g. Josephus, *Ant.* 3.120). Similarly, in the NT, *lovers of money* occurs only here and Luke 16.14, of Jesus' opponents, with the noun in the description of false teachers in I Tim. 6.10, cf. IV Macc. 2.8.
Boastful There are several parallels in vocabulary between this section and the list of vicious people in Rom. 1.30–31, as with this word, cf. also the noun in James 4.16; I John 2.16; Job 28.8; Philo, *Moses* 2.240; Josephus, *Ant.* 8.264.
Arrogant cf. Rom. 1.30; Luke 1.51; James 4.6; I Peter 5.5; Prov. 3.34.
Abusive/slanderous cf. the description of Paul's former life in I Tim. 1.13.
Disobedient to parents cf. Rom. 1.30. This is the opposite of the depiction of Paul and Timothy in 1.3, 5.
Devoid of gratitude is found only here and Luke 6.35 in the NT, but it is

often denounced in Hellenistic literature (e.g. Epictetus 2.23.5; Wisd. 16.29; IV Macc 9.10; Philo, *Joseph* 99; Josephus, *Ant.* 13.388).

3.3 *Devoid of piety* is literally *unholy* cf. I Tim. 1.9.

Devoid of natural affection occurs only here and Rom. 1.31 in the NT.

Implacable in their hatreds is also found only here and Rom. 1.31 in the NT, cf. Philo, *On the virtues* 131; *Moses* 1.242; Josephus, *Ant.* 4.264.

Scandalmongers/slanderers cf. I Tim. 3.11 where women are warned against the vice. The word is used both for the devil (2.26) and for critical outsiders (I Tim. 3.7).

Uncontrolled see the cognate noun in I Cor. 7.5.

Violent/untamed only here in the NT, cf. Epictetus 1.3.7.

Hostile to all goodness occurs only here in ancient Greek literature. It represents a disposition which precludes what the Pastorals demand, good deeds.

3.4 *Perfidious* occurs only here and Luke 6.16, of Judas; Acts 7.52 in the NT, cf. Philo, *Special Laws* 3.164; Josephus, *War* 3.354.

Foolhardy is found only here and Acts 19.36 in the NT, cf. Prov. 10.14; 13.3; Josephus, *Ant.* 5.106.

Swollen with self-importance cf. I Tim. 3.6; 6.14.

Love their pleasures is literally *loving pleasure*, which occurs only here in the NT, cf. Dio Chrysostom 4.115; Philo, *Husbandry* 88; *loving God* is also found only here in the NT, cf. Philo, ibid. 88.

3.5 *While preserving the outward form of religion, they are a standing denial of its power*. *Religion* interprets *piety*, the most important virtue, according to the Pastorals (e.g. I Tim. 3.16; 4.7). Moreover, the Pastorals teach that power belongs to God (1.7–8). For similar complaints see I Tim. 6.5–6; Philo, *Noah as a Planter* 70.

Keep clear occurs only here in the NT, cf. IV Macc. 1.33.

3.6 *Silly women* is literally *little women* but used in a derogatory sense. This is the only instance in the NT, but the contempt for women which it expresses was common in Hellenistic literature, cf. Epictetus, *Enchiridion* 7.

Carried away only here in the NT, cf. Polybius 16.8.9.

All kinds of desires Desires is the same Greek word which was translated *passions* in 2.22.

3.7 *Knowledge of the truth* cf. 2.25; I Tim. 2.4; 4.3.

3.8 *Warped minds* is another instance of a word without parallel in the rest of the NT.

Disqualify them is literally the adjective *disqualified* cf. Rom. 1.28, of all pagans who do not acknowledge God; I Cor. 9.27; Titus 1.16.

3.9 *Fools* is used only here and Luke 6.11 in the NT; cf. Josephus, *War* 2.110.

Paul's example, the counter-example of charlatans, and a further appeal for Timothy's fidelity
3.10–17

3.10–13   The description of the vicious character of people in the last days is followed by a contrasting reflection on the manner of Paul's life. Timothy is reminded that he has followed closely not only Paul's teaching but also his practice of the teaching through dispositions which express a particular way of living. That good teaching is to be enacted in exemplary behaviour was commonly accepted in Jewish and Greek Hellenistic literature (cf. I Tim. 4.6; Epictetus 2.9.13). Hence Paul's *resolution* is said to have issued in *faithfulness, patience, love and endurance* or *fortitude.* This last virtue is stressed throughout the epistle because Paul is characterised as someone who had faced *persecutions and sufferings,* some of which are briefly recalled (cf. II Cor. 11.23–33, although the exact locations mentioned in II Tim. are not parallel). That *the Lord had rescued* Paul encourages both Timothy (1.8; 2.3) and *everyone who wants to live a godly life as a follower of Jesus* to endure the sufferings which persecution would involve. Paul is understood to have experienced and to be still experiencing persecutions for no other reason than his preaching of the faith (1.12), and this means that his faithful associates like Timothy, and now even ordinary followers, are called to share in the suffering (cf. Phil. 1.29). Not all, however, are expected to face martyrdom like Paul (4.6–8). As the Lord had rescued Paul in the past, an echo of Ps. 34.17, so Timothy and other believers might also be rescued. But suffering persecution is presented as a mark of fidelity, as in II Cor. 11–12. Only *evil-doers and charlatans will progress from bad to worse, deceiving and deceived.* In I Tim. 4.15, Timothy had been urged to make exemplary progress in the virtues. Here, charlatans are also reckoned to make progress, but in the opposite direction, from bad to worse. That they are deceiving others is explained by their being deceived themselves (cf. I Tim. 4.1–2; 6.20). Deception is the opposite of the knowledge of the truth which the epistle encourages (2.25; 3.7–8). They are presented as the kind of people no one should follow. On the contrary, Timothy is to *stand by* the things he has *learned* and *is assured of*, through his recollection of Paul's example.

3.14–17 Moreover, Timothy is to draw on another source of guidance. He is assured that his knowledge of *the sacred scriptures* (cf. Philo, *Moses* 2.292), gained from early childhood (cf. 1.5), would *make* him *wise*, not for any worldly profit, but for *salvation through faith in Christ Jesus*. Here *salvation* could be understood as present or future or both. The allusions to the Jewish Scriptures in 2.19 and 3.8–9 have already indicated something of their worth. Now they are said to be *inspired by God*. Reflection has led both to a definition of the source of these scriptures' authority and to a list of the matters for which they are deemed useful. That they are *inspired by God* is such a common belief among Christians that it is a surprise to discover how singular is this particular description. It is without exact parallel in either contemporary Jewish or Christian literature, although Josephus asserts that the prophets who wrote the biblical histories owed their knowledge to God (*Against Apion* 1.37). Moreover, Hellenistic philosophical writings regard their philosophies as inspired by God (e.g. Plutarch, *Mor.* 904F). The description serves to explain why these scriptures are considered useful *for teaching* (REB's *the truth* is an interpretive addition to the text), *for reproof* (REB *refuting error*), *for improvement* (REB *for reformation of manners*), and *for discipline* in *justice* or *righteousness* (REB *right living*). These were the purposes served by the allusions to the scriptures in 2.19; 3.8–9 (cf. I Cor. 10.1–6). The Pastorals' concern for healthy teaching and for the justice and love which it should engender determines the way in which the scriptures' usefulness is conceived. Even so, some of the teachings of these scriptures, for example, on the release of slaves (I Tim. 6.1–2), are ignored. Nevertheless, these uses of scripture are said to serve the purpose of enabling *the man* or woman *of God* (cf. Deut. 33.1 of Moses) to be *capable and equipped for good work of every kind*, the purpose also of the epistle's teaching (2.21).

This chapter, therefore, provides the reader with graphic examples of how to live well and of what to avoid. Paul's good example inspires imitation, even in sharing his suffering, while the bad examples of both present and future characters create the kind of aversion which reinforces the worth of the positive exemplar. The epistle had made use of the Jewish Scriptures for warning and encouragement, and this use is formally justified in a recommendation that the reader should go on drawing strength from that inspired source.

Notes on 3.10–17

As usual, the teaching is expressed in distinctive vocabulary:

3.10 *Manner of life* is found only here in the NT; cf. Esth. 2.20; II Macc. 11.24; Josephus, *Ant.* 14.195.

Resolution is used of human beings only here and Acts 11.23; 27.13 in the NT. III Macc 5.29; Rom. 8.28; II Tim. 1.9 use the word to refer to God's purpose.

3.13 *Charlatans* is found only here in the NT, cf. Dio Chrysostom 15.11; Philo, *Special Laws* 1.315; Josephus, *Ant.* 20.97.

Deceiving and deceived cf. Dio Chrysostom 48.10.

3.15 *Make wise* occurs only here and II Peter 1.16 in the NT, cf. Diog. L. 5.90.

3.16 *Improvement* (REB *Reformation of manners*) The word was often used in Hellenistic writings to recommend the improvement which philosophical reflection would bring, e.g. Plutarch, *On listening to lectures* 16, *Mor.* 46D; Epictetus 3.21.15. Here, the only instance of its use in the NT, it is integrated into the theological ethics of the epistle by attributing such improvement to the scriptures inspired by God.

Discipline in justice or *right living* contrast Rom. 3.21–22; Gal. 3.6.

Capable is found only here in the NT; cf. Epictetus 1.28.3.

Equipped in this sense is used only here in the NT; cf. Diodorus Siculus 14.19.

3.11 The association of Paul's persecutions with particular places is also found in Acts:

Antioch cf. Acts 13.45–50; 14.19–21.

Iconium cf. Acts 14.2–5, 19.

Lystra cf. Acts 14.19.

Acts, however, sets Paul's meeting with Timothy after these events (Acts 16.1–3), whereas II Tim. creates the impression that Timothy had been present on the occasions mentioned.

The Final Appeal to Timothy

4.1–8

4.1 The appeal is expressed with all the solemnity of a final testament, and reminds Timothy of the presence of God and of Christ Jesus (see 2.14; I Tim. 5.21). Moreover, Jesus is described as the one *who is to judge the living and the dead*. According to I Peter 4.5, God would judge the living and the dead, but here emphasis is placed on Jesus' role. The man whose fidelity involved a martyr's death (2.11) is to act as God's agent at the judgment. The reference also implies that some people would be still alive at the eschaton, but does not state that Timothy or any other believers of that generation would be among them. Certainly, 4.6–8 implies that Paul would not be among them (cf. Phil. 1.19–26 and contrast I Cor. 15.51–52). This focus on the coming eschatological judgment implicitly counters the belief that resurrection has happened already (2.18), and it also forces the reader to remember that fidelity and endurance are required in the present if believers are to live with Christ at the eschaton (2.12–13).

Hence mention is explicitly made of both Jesus' appearing (which here refers to his future eschatological appearing, REB *his coming appearance;* contrast his past appearing: 1.10, and compare I Tim. 6.14), and his *kingdom* (REB *reign).* This is the first reference to Christ's kingdom in the Pastorals. In 4.18, the only other instance, this kingdom is defined as a *heavenly kingdom.* In I Cor. 6.9 and 15.50, reference is made to the kingdom of God, but I Cor. 15.24 suggests that, in the future, Christ would deliver the kingdom to God after destroying every rule and every authority and power, asserting that 'he (Christ) must reign until he has put all his enemies under his feet', and specifying that the last enemy is death. This explains why believers would be raised only at the eschaton. Further, Eph. 5.5 refers to the kingdom of God and of Christ, and Col. 1.13 refers to the kingdom of his (God's) son. Since Jesus is given the role of judge as God's agent in II Tim. 4.1, it is appropriate that the kingdom should be described as his. But is the reader to envisage this heavenly kingdom as the immediate destination of martyrs like Paul? It seems not, since 4.8 pictures Paul's receipt of his crown of righteousness at the future eschatological judgment. In spite of the confession of Christ's present universal triumph in I Tim. 3.16, and in spite of the assertion that Jesus Christ abolished death at his first appearing (1.10), therefore, II Tim. seems to reflect the same expectations as those in I Cor. 15, except that now Paul's death is expected before the eschaton. Of course, this distinction between the time of someone's death and the time of the same person's resurrection can only be made from the perspective of a continuing human world in which time is conceived in terms of past, present and future. The Pastorals confess belief in the eternal God whose existence is not historical but transcendent and look forward to eternal life for faithful believers. These opening statements of the final appeal to Timothy encourage him to understand the present in terms of the expectation of Christ's future appearing and the eschatological judgment.

4.2–5 This perspective, as well as the reference to apostasy in verse 3, explains why Timothy's preaching should be offered *in season and out of season*. The expression is an emphatic oxymoron. Hellenistic philosophical literature frequently advises teachers about choosing the appropriate manner and the appropriate occasion for giving insights to others, in order to persuade people effectively. That Timothy is instructed to proclaim the message even when the time is unfavourable stands out as unusual (see A. J. Malherbe, 1984). Nevertheless, the manner in which Timothy is urged to teach conforms to Hellenistic advice. *Argument, reproof and appeal* are to be offered *with all the patience that teaching requires* (cf. 2.24–25; 3.10). An unfavourable time in the future for teaching is then described. People would not respond to the *healthy teaching* which the epistle claims to encapsulate, with its reproofs as well as exhortations, and with its emphasis on endurance of sufferings, but would be looking for the kinds of teachers who would indulge their own whims and fancies. The Greek text uses the expression *itching ears* to convey the insatiable and superficial nature of their desires (cf. Plutarch, *Superstition* 5, *Mor.* 167B). So, they can be charged with stopping their ears to *the truth*, that is, to the truth about God's purpose as understood by the epistle (cf. 2.15, 18, 25; 3.7, 8). Instead, they are represented as turning to *fables or myths*. This is the only reference to myths in II Tim. (cf. I Tim. 1.4; 4.7; Titus 1.14; II Peter 1.16), and the myths are neither described nor refuted. Polybius refers disparagingly to the public's liking myths, which he distinguishes from his own historical narrative (9.2.1). These future believers, then, are pictured as sharing this deplored fondness. Whatever happens, however, Timothy is to *keep* his *head* or *remain sober* (cf. the same image in 2.26). Moreover, he is to *put up with hardship* as Paul is described doing (2.9). Even hardship is not to discourage him from *doing the work of an evangelist* (REB *work to spread the gospel*). In Eph. 4.11, Christ is said to give to God's people evangelists, together with apostles, prophets, pastors and teachers, and in Acts 21.8, Philip is called an evangelist. The noun has the same Greek root as the verb *to announce* or *proclaim* and as the abstract noun *good news* or *gospel*. Perhaps surprisingly, therefore, these are the only three instances of its use in the NT. In summary, Timothy is urged to *fulfil your service* (REB *discharge all the duties of your calling*). Timothy's task, and all it involves, is conceived as service to God and Christ, as well as to the community of believers (cf. I Tim. 4.6).

4.6–7 Timothy's fidelity is represented as crucial in view of the expectation that Paul himself would soon be martyred. In this, too, the portrait of Paul provides an example of quiet endurance. The translation *my life is already being poured out on the altar* seeks to express the sense of the Greek verb which usually refers to pouring out drink offerings or libations (e.g. Ex 25.29; 30.9). Here, as in Phil. 2.17, it is metaphorical, referring to Paul's sufferings and imminent death for the faith in fidelity to God's purpose. *The hour* or *time of my departure is upon me* is also a metaphorical reference to his death, as in Philo (*Against Flaccus* 187). The noun *departure* is found only here in the NT but the cognate verb is used for the same purpose in Phil. 1.23. Reflection on Paul's past is presented in athletic metaphors of boxing and running to convey the sense of Paul's strenuous but purposeful work. *Struggled in the good contest* is a better translation than REB's *run the great race* (cf. I Tim. 6.12; I Cor. 9.25; Phil. 2.16) because the expression highlights the hardship Paul endured. The second metaphor understands Paul's *course* as now *complete* (cf. Philo, *Allegorical Interpretation* 3.48 and the similar metaphors in Phil. 2.16; 3.13–14). Proleptically, his martyrdom is assumed. And throughout, Paul is said to have *kept the faith*, as Timothy is encouraged to do (1.13–14, cf. I Tim. 6.20).

4.8 Finally, the focus moves from Paul's imminent martyrdom to his vindication at the eschaton (cf. 4.1). *There awaits me* expresses the certainty of the expectation. *The garland* or *crown* was customarily awarded to the winner of athletic contests, but here it is defined as the crown *of righteousness* or *justice,* the recognition for a just or righteous life (cf. 2.22; 3.16; I Cor. 9.25). This reward would be given to Paul by *the Lord,* probably a reference to Christ Jesus as the Lord of believers (cf. 4.1; 1.2), who is called *the just* or *righteous judge,* who thus encourages justice among his servants. *On that day* (REB interprets *on the great day*) refers to the day of judgment (cf. I Cor. 5.5; I Thess. 5.2). Moreover, reward would then be given not only to Paul but also to *all who have loved his appearing* (REB interprets *all who have set their hearts on his coming appearance).* The REB understands this reference to Jesus' appearing as future, as in 4.1, but it could refer to his past appearing (1.10), love of which would encourage the fidelity which is said to ensure the reward (2.11–13). The reference to all faithful believers shows the relevance of Paul's example for Timothy and for all those he would teach. This moving portrait of Paul as a man who has faithfully endured such hardships for his beliefs and just practices, and who faces martyrdom with equanimity in the certainty of a just eschatological judgment and reward, not only forms a fitting conclusion to the epistle's teaching, but also serves to guarantee its trustworthiness.

Notes on 4.1–8

Again, the passage includes distinctive vocabulary:

4.3 *Follow a crowd of teachers* is literally *accumulate teachers.* The verb is found only here in the NT, cf. Epictetus 1.10.5.

4.4 *Turn to* In the NT, the verb is used only in the Pastorals, cf. I Tim. 1.6; 5.15; 6.20; Epictetus 1.6.42; Philo, *Special Laws* 2.23; Josephus, *Ant.* 8.251.

4.5 *Put up with hardship* is the same verb as that used in 2.9 of Paul's suffering. In the NT, it occurs only in the Pastorals and in James 5.13; cf. Jonah 4.10; Philo, *On the virtues* 88; Josephus, *Ant.* 10.220.

The mutual support of loyal associates contrasted with the disloyalty of some others
4.9–22

Among those scholars who argue that the Pastorals were not written by the historical Paul, some have suggested that, nevertheless, they include some genuine fragments of Pauline letters. This passage is always included among those genuine fragments, though there are various hypotheses about the allocation of particular verses among the reconstructed letters. The reference *apart from Luke, I have no one with me*, it is argued, contradicts the reference to those who send greetings in 4.21, and the two verses must therefore come from two different fragmentary Pauline letters (e.g. Harrison 1921 and 1964; Barrett 1963). The main reason for suggesting that this section and other references to travel plans and greetings (I Tim. 3.14; Titus 3.12–15) represent fragments from genuine Pauline letters, however, is that no other rhetorical purpose could be discerned for including such relatively mundane matters in pseudepigraphical epistles. But Donelson (1986) has shown how common were these types of references in Hellenistic pseudepigraphical letters. He discerns two rhetorical purposes that they serve in such literature. The first is to create the impression that the pseudepigraphical letter is actually genuine. References to possessions (4.13), for example, impress the reader with their realism. The second is to express the sense of a community of associates who cared for each other, and who, therefore, put into practice the teaching which the epistle advocates. This only means, however, that the question about the possible authorship of the Pastorals has to be argued on other criteria (see the appendix).

4.9–12   REB's *do your best* is better translated *hasten* (also 4.21; Titus 3.12), one of the verb's possible meanings, since the preceding section had emphasised the imminence of Paul's martyrdom.

Timothy is being urged to imitate Onesiphorus (1.16–17) rather than Demas (cf. Philemon 24; Col. 4.14), whose desertion is explained in terms of his *loving the present age* (cf. I Tim. 6.17 where the present age is also mentioned; REB interprets *his heart set on this present world*). II Tim. 4.1, 8 had already directed the reader's attention beyond the present age to the eschatological judgment and kingdom. The absence of Crescens, who is mentioned only here in the NT, and of Titus (cf. Titus 1.4) does not imply their desertion too but suggests that they are serving the Pauline mission elsewhere. *Apart from Luke, I have no one with me* literally reads *Luke alone is with me*, presumably in Rome (1.17). In Philemon 24, Luke is mentioned as one of Paul's fellow-workers who sent greetings in that letter from prison, along with Mark, Aristarchus and Demas (cf. Col. 4.14). The reference adds piquancy to the request that Timothy hasten to Paul. But how is it to be reconciled with the greetings sent from all the brothers in 4.21? A distinction seems to be drawn between Paul's close associates in his mission, among whom are Luke and Timothy, and the others mentioned in these few verses, and ordinary members of the local church in Rome, who send greetings at the end of the epistle. The suggestion that Timothy should bring Mark because he is *useful for service* (cf. 2.21; REB *a great help to me*), encourages Timothy's service too (4.5). Curiously, there is no hint about where Timothy would find Mark. Paul's sending Tychicus (cf. Titus 3.12; Eph. 6.21; Col. 4.7; Acts 20.4) to Ephesus, where Timothy has been staying (1:18; 4.19), seems to imply that he would take over Timothy's responsibilities in that city so that Timothy could obey the instruction that he go to Paul in Rome. These references to particular people and their whereabouts suggest that Paul is at the centre of a network of associates, only one of whom had deserted him during his imprisonment.

4.13   Next come instructions to Timothy about Paul's belongings. *Bring the cloak I left with Carpus at Troas* is explained by the later urging of Timothy to join Paul before winter (4.21). Cloaks were used as bed covers in winter, as well as for outdoor wear. No explanation is offered of its being left at Troas, but the reference to Carpus implies that community members could be trusted to look after the property of other believers. Where Timothy would find *the books and notebooks*, what they contained, and why Paul wanted them remains unclear. Like the epistle itself, however, this reference declares that Paul is a scholar. Moreover, the earlier impression of the immediacy of Paul's martyrdom (4.6–7) is now understood as proleptic. Timothy should hasten to Paul, and should journey before winter, when travel was even more hazardous and uncertain than at other times (4.21), but such a journey from Ephesus to Rome, even in the best circumstances, would take months, especially with visits to pick up Mark, the cloak from Carpus, and the books, and yet Paul looks forward to their joyous reunion before his death (1.4).

4.14–18   After these detailed arrangements, the epistle recalls Paul's recent experiences for Timothy's benefit. Alexander the coppersmith may or may not be the same Alexander as the person mentioned in I Tim. 1.20, since Alexander was a common name. If he is the same character, the reform sought in I Tim. is now understood to have failed. *The great deal of harm* he is said to have done Paul is unspecified, but it is assumed that Paul's opponents would also be Timothy's. No retaliatory action against Alexander, however, is encouraged. Rather, confidence is expressed that *the Lord will deal with him as he deserves*, presumably at the final judgment (4.1, cf. Rom. 2.6). *At my first defence* (REB *at the first hearing of my case*) seems to refer to that mentioned in Phil. 1.7, 16. *No one came into court to support me* provokes the reader's consternation and sympathy. *I pray that it may not be counted against them*, again at the final judgment (4.1), conveys a spirit of forbearance (cf. 2.24–25). Moreover, the acknowledgement that *the Lord stood by me and gave me strength* recalls the earlier teaching that only God's power could help people to remain faithful during persecution (1.8–14, cf. Phil. 4.13). This empowerment is represented as allowing Paul to make *a full proclamation of the gospel for the whole pagan world* (literally, *all the nations) to hear*. This could refer either to the whole of Paul's mission to the Gentiles (cf. I Tim. 3.6; Rom. 1.5; 11.25), as seems more likely, or to all the Gentiles present at the trial. *Rescued from the lion's jaws* is a metaphor for rescue from danger in general, rather than to an expected execution through combat with lions in the arena (cf. Ps. 22.21). This past rescue, however, is not expected to be repeated in the future. Rather, in the imminent future, Paul expects to be saved, not for further missionary work, but for *the Lord's heavenly kingdom*, at the eschaton (see 4.8). Fittingly, the verse ends with praise of this Lord: *glory to him for ever and ever! Amen*.

4.19–22   The customary conclusion of Hellenistic epistles is adapted for a Christian purpose, as in other NT epistles. Greetings are sent to and from believers, and a final grace concludes the whole work.

Prisca and Aquila are mentioned in I Cor. 16.19, where they are linked with the churches of Asia, the province in which Ephesus was situated. Greetings sent to the household of Onesiphorus suggest both that Onesiphorus himself is understood not yet to have returned from Rome (see 1.16–18), and that his household supported his mission there. That Erastus (cf. Rom. 16.23) has stayed at Corinth and that Trophimus has been left ill at Miletus explains why no greetings are sent from them. This mention of Trophimus' illness also highlights one of the dangers of missionary work (cf. I Tim. 5.23), but the Pastorals never refer to miraculous healings (contrast I Cor. 12.9, 28). *Do try to get here before winter* (see 4.13 above) expresses both concern for Timothy's well-being and Paul's longing to see him. None of the names of the people from whom greetings are sent in 4.21 occur elsewhere in the NT. The form of the final grace shares only some elements with those at the end of other Paulines. *With your spirit* conforms to Gal. 6.18; Phil. 4.23. *Grace be with you* (plural) is identical to I Tim. 6.21. In spite of the address to Timothy alone throughout the epistle, this plural ending recognises that the teaching is to be passed on and implemented by a wider audience of believers. Perhaps it even implies that the epistle itself should be read at a community meeting.

Notes on 4.9–15

4.10 *Galatia* in Asia Minor or modern Turkey is also mentioned in Gal. 1.2; I Cor. 16.1; I Peter 1.1.
Dalmatia in southern Illyricum, across the Adriatic Sea from Italy, is mentioned only here in the NT.
4.13 *The cloak* This is a Latin loan word which occurs only here in the NT, cf. Epictetus 4.8.34.
Troas is mentioned as a place where Paul preached in II Cor. 2.12, cf. Acts 16.8, 11; 20.5–6.
Books The word can also mean *scrolls*, cf. Isa. 34.4; Gal. 3.10.
The notebooks is literally *parchments*, a Latin loan word used only here in the NT.
4.16 *came into court to support me* is literally *stood by* or *came to the aid of*. It is used in this sense only here in the NT, cf. Plato, *Republic* 2.368B.
4.20 *Trophimus* Elsewhere, he is mentioned only in Acts 20.4; 21.29, where he is pictured as a native of Ephesus.

TITUS

Outline

Paul, the exemplary teacher, reminds Titus that he had been left behind in Crete to appoint blameless elders who would silence insubordinate opponents. The epistle then gives further instructions to Titus, about the appropriate behaviour that he should encourage among older and younger men and women, and slaves, including exhortation that he should become a model for younger men to follow. The teaching emphasises that it is God's grace which saves people, and suggests that present salvation is to be understood as a period of training. Additional instructions concern believers' relations with outsiders, and highlight the change involved in becoming a believer. Finally, attention is given to Titus' behaviour towards ordinary members of the community and towards opponents.

An introductory reminder of why Titus was left in Crete
1.1–16

1.1–4 The salutation mentions not only who Paul is but also what his mission entails, as in Rom. 1.1–6. He is called a *servant* or *slave of God* (cf. II Tim. 2.24; James 1.1), understanding his ministry as fulfilling God's purpose. As in I Tim. 1.1 and II Tim. 1.1, he is also called *apostle of Jesus Christ*, a person Christ sent, although the more usual order in the Pastorals, *Christ Jesus*, is found in the other two epistles. His minstry is said to accord with *the faith of God's chosen people*. In some other Paulines, the salutation insists that believers share a common faith (Rom. 1.1–6; I Cor. 1.2), and Rom. 8.33 and Col. 3.12 also call believers God's chosen people (cf. II Tim. 2.10), a designation of the Jewish people in the Jewish Scriptures (e.g. I Chron. 16.13; Ps. 105.6; Isa. 42.1; 43.20; 45.4). What is distinctive of the Pastorals, however, is the definition of this faith as *the knowledge of the truth* (cf. I Tim. 2.4; 4.3; II Tim. 2.25; 3.7), although other Paulines call the good news *the truth* (Gal. 2.5, 14; 5.7; II Cor. 13.8; II Thess. 2.10). As usual, the REB interprets *piety* as *religion*, another concept found only in the Pastorals among the epistles attributed to Paul. Ancient Greek literature has no word for *religion*, but reckons *piety* as one of the cardinal virtues. This virtue, however, is given even greater stress in the theological ethics of the Pastorals, as in Hellenistic Judaism.

Moreover, the salutation gives one part of the common faith special prominence: *the hope of eternal life*. I Tim.'s salutation had referred more briefly to Christ Jesus as *our hope*, but had gone on to mention *eternal life* as the content of the hope (I Tim 1.1, 16). Since that hope rests on trust in God's promise, assurance is given that *God does not lie*. It seems odd that a need is felt to express the assurance in these terms, but Philo does the same in *Drunkenness* 139. No citation from the Jewish Scriptures justifies the claim that God promised eternal life *long ages ago* (cf. II Tim. 1.9). The only place where eternal life is specifically mentioned in those Scriptures is Dan 12.2, but other passages, like Gen. 2–3 or Ezek. 37, could be interpreted to imply such a promise. REB's *in his own good time* interprets *at its own time.* This reassuring assertion about God's providential timing of events had been used in connexion with both Jesus' historical appearing (I Tim. 2.6) and his eschatological appearing (I Tim. 6.15). Now it is connected with *the proclamation* of God's purpose, a proclamation said to have been *entrusted* to Paul (cf. II Tim. 4.17) *by command of God our Saviour,* an expression used to explain Paul's apostleship in I Tim. 1.1. That God is to be understood as *Saviour* will be justified later in the epistle (2.11–14). This salutation, therefore, presents Paul, not as exemplary martyr (II Tim. 1.8–12), nor as the greatest of sinners (I Tim. 1.12–17), but as exemplary teacher.

Titus is mentioned elsewhere in the Paulines as Paul's metaphorical brother (II Cor. 2.13), partner and fellow-worker (II Cor. 8.23), a Greek, whom Paul and Barnabas had taken to Jerusalem (Gal. 2.1, 3). He is said to have joined Paul in Macedonia after a visit to Corinth and to have given a good report of that community's obedience (II Cor. 7.6–16). He is also expected to return there to facilitate the collection for believers in Jerusalem (II Cor. 8.6, 16–17; 12.18). II Tim. 4.10 relates that he was visiting Dalmatia. Titus is never mentioned in Acts. According to this epistle, Paul had left him on the island of Crete (1.5). Like Timothy (I Tim. 1.2), he is addressed as Paul's *loyal or legitimate child* because he can be assumed to share Paul's faith, in contrast to the *undisciplined people* who will be mentioned in 1.10. To him, *grace and peace* are sent, according to most older manuscripts, although many later manuscripts include *mercy,* as in I Tim. 1.2; II Tim. 1.2. Like the other Pastorals, the grace and peace sent to Titus by Paul are said to come from *God the Father and from Christ Jesus,* but in I and II Tim., Christ is called *our Lord,* whereas here he is called *our Saviour.* Again, this description will be justified in 2.11–14.

1.5–6 The rest of this chapter recalls the purpose for which Titus was left in Crete, and, in that way, sets the scene for the instructions which follow. In the NT, *Crete* is mentioned only here and in Acts 27.7–15, as a place past which a ship carrying Paul to Rome was sailing. Here, a successful Pauline mission in Crete is assumed, after which Titus had been left behind to *deal with any outstanding matters,* and, in particular, to *appoint elders in each town.* REB's *in accordance with the principles I have laid down* paraphrases *as I directed you*, understanding the clause to refer to the instructions which follow. This is a possible interpretation, but the clause could simply refer back to Paul's command about appointing elders. For a discussion of *elders* and their possible relationship to other community leaders, see the commentary of I Tim. 3.1–13; 4.14; 5.17–22. As in I Tim. 3, the instructions first focus on the character of these elders, rather than on their particular responsibilities. Unusually, the REB construes the list of virtues which follow as a series of questions, which is a possible rendering of the introductory Greek particle, otherwise understood as conditional. In general terms, Titus is advised to appoint as an elder a man who is *unimpeachable* (cf. I Tim. 3.10 of deacons). What this involves is then spelt out. *A husband of one wife* is also required of overseer and deacon in I Tim. 3.2, 12 (see the commentary there). That his children should be *believers* is assumed of the leaders described in I Tim. 3. Moreover, as believers, these children should live orderly lives, *not open to any charge of dissipation or indiscipline*. A charge of indiscipline had been made against false teachers in I Tim. 1.9. Elders, then, are to be free, married men, who manage their families well (cf. I Tim. 3.4–5, 12, of overseer and deacons).

1.7–8 The connexion *for* implies that *elder* and *overseer* (REB *bishop*) are to be identified, as does the repetition of the adjective *unimpeachable*. *Overseer*, therefore, briefly indicates the role which the elder should play. Moreover, the requirement that he should be unimpeachable is explained by calling him *God's house-steward*. In I Cor. 4.1, Paul had described himself and other missionaries as stewards of God's mysteries who should be trustworthy. Here, the overseer is conceived as the manager of God's household, resident in the local community of believers (cf. I Tim. 3.15). The kinds of faults to be avoided by house-stewards in general, and by God's house-steward in particular, are then listed: *not overbearing or short-tempered or given to drink*　(cf. I Tim. 3.3 of overseer), *no brawler* (cf. I Tim. 3.3 of an overseer), *no money grubber* (cf. I Tim. 3.8 of deacons). On the contrary, he is to be: *hospitable* (cf. I Tim. 3.2 of the overseer), *right-minded* or *a lover of goodness, temperate* (cf. I Tim. 3.2 of the overseer), *just* (one of the cardinal Greek virtues), *devout or holy* (cf. I Tim. 1.9 which describes false teachers as exhibiting the contrary vice), *self-controlled* (cf. Gal. 5.23, among the fruits of the Spirit, another cardinal virtue among the Greeks, e.g. Aristotle, *Eth. Nic.* 7.4). This character sketch of a moderate man, in control of his passions, is similar to that of leaders in I Tim. 3 and to that of other leaders in Hellenistic literature. The teaching is grounded theologically by the reference to God's steward and by the implied assumption that the church is God's household. Here, however, new converts are not excluded, as they are in I Tim. 3.6, because this epistle depicts a situation in which all believers would be new converts.

1.9 A specifically Christian characteristic is then added to this conventionally acceptable sketch: *he must keep a firm hold on the sure statement as taught* (REB paraphrases *of the true doctrine*). The reason for this demand is then explained: *so that he may be well able both to appeal (to his hearers) with sound* or *healthy teaching and to refute those who raise objections*. Once again, the medical metaphor, which describes teaching as healthy or diseased, is employed (cf. I Tim. 1.10). All these elders/overseers, then, are to be appointed to teach (cf. I Tim. 3.2, which requires the overseer to be a good teacher, and I Tim. 5.17, which assumes that some elders would preach and teach). Elders, it seems, are to be appointed to perform those tasks most necessary for the well-being of a particular community, and, in a community of new converts, teaching would be of prime importance.

1.10–11 Moreover, what a good teacher is receives further definition by a contrasting depiction of bad teachers. The REB omits the introductory *for*, which makes the connexion with the preceding advice. REB's *Jewish converts* interprets the phrase: *those of the circumcision*, a group opposed in Gal. 2.12, but, whereas Galatians seeks to refute their views by argument, the epistle to Titus offers no counterarguments. Rather, the group is simply denigrated in terms conventionally used in Hellenistic literature of opposing teachers. They are called *undisciplined*, a vice excluded for the children of those to be appointed as elders in 1.6. They are said to *talk wildly, lead others astray* (REB's interpretation of *deceivers*), *teach what they should not* (cf. I Tim. 5.13 of gossiping widows), and *for sordid gain* (cf. I Tim. 3.8; 6.5). For these reasons, they are to be *muzzled, because they are ruining whole families or households*. Similar reasons for opposing bad teachers are given in II Tim. 2.18 and 3.6. In other words, these bad teachers exhibit the vices which God's steward should avoid.

1.12–16 A link is then made with the Cretan context by citing a saying about the bad character of Cretans by a Cretan *prophet: Cretans were ever liars, vicious brutes, lazy gluttons*. Clement of

Alexandria (*Strom.* 1.59.2) attributes the saying to Epimenides of Crete. *Liars* connects with *deceivers* in verse 10, and perhaps *vicious brutes* with *undisciplined*, and *lazy gluttons* with *for sordid gain*. Of course, attributing a true saying to a Cretan (liar) is paradoxical, and such paradoxes were commonly discussed by Greek philosphers (see A. T. Thiselton, 1994). It is unlikely, therefore, that the author missed the irony. Titus' role, in *rebuking* such people, is the same as that to be played by the overseer in 1.9, but now its purpose is explained in different terms: *so that they may be restored to a sound faith*, or, more literally, *so that they may be made well in the faith*, a slight variation on the usual use of the medical metaphor. Whereas earlier advice (1.11) suggested that bad teachers were to be muzzled to prevent their upsetting others, now the purpose of opposing them is related to their own welfare, as in I Tim. 1.20; II Tim. 2.25–26. Since these teachers had earlier been called *those of the circumcision* (1.10), the *myths* (cf. I Tim. 1.4; II Tim. 4.4) to which they are said to *pay heed* are defined as *Jewish myths*, presumably about Abraham, and *human commandments* may refer to those which require circumcision. *Turning their backs on* or *away from the truth* is a typical complaint against false teachers in the Pastorals (II Tim. 2.18; 4.4). *To the pure all things are pure* is a truism shared with Philo (*Special Laws* 3.208–209). I Tim. 1.5 and 3.9 had emphasised the need for a pure heart and a pure conscience. In other words, purity is understood in ethical terms, as sometimes in the Jewish Scriptures (e.g. Ps. 24.4). The truism is developed, both by specifying its opposite: *nothing is pure to the tainted and disbelievers, but both their mind and their conscience are tainted*, and by making a connexion between belief and practice, a connexion frequently made in contemporary Hellenistic and Jewish literature: *they profess to know God but by their actions deny him* (cf. II Tim. 3.5). That their understanding is corrupt, and that their conscience, which should have provided a final brake on bad actions, is also corrupt (cf. I Tim. 1.19; 4.2), is exhibited in their unethical behaviour, specified in the preceding lists of vices. Hence they are reckoned to be *detestable and disobedient*, like the people described as present in the last days (II Tim. 3.2), and *disqualified for any good work*, that is, for the good works which the epistle requires all believers to perform (3.1).

Recalling Titus' past responsibility to appoint blameless elders who could join with him in refuting the insubordinate and corrupt in order to curtail their influence and effect their reform, provides the background to the rest of the epistle's exhortation. The positive and negative character sketches, with their alliterative and assonant lists of virtues and vices, moreover, encourage the reader's imitation or avoidance.

Notes on Titus 1.1–16

As in the case of the other Pastorals, this epistle contains some vocabulary which is distinctive within the Pauline corpus, and which is typical of Hellenistic writings:

1.1 *Servant* or *slave of God* Contrast *slave of Jesus Christ* in Rom. 1.1; Gal. 1.10; Phil. 1.1; Col. 4.12.

1.5 *Deal with* or *put in order* occurs only here in the NT, cf. Philo, *Against Flaccus* 124.

1.7 *Not overbearing* is used only here and II Peter 2.10 in the NT, cf. Prov. 21.19.

1.8 *Right minded* or *lover of goodness* is found only here in the NT, cf. Wisd. 7.22.

1.9 *Keep firm hold,* in this sense, occurs only here in the Paulines.

1.10 *Talk wildly* or *idle talkers* The adjective is found only here in the NT but the cognate noun is used in I Tim. 1.6.
Lead others astray or *deceivers* is found only here in the NT but the cognate verb is used in Gal. 6.3.

1.11 *Muzzled* occurs only here in the NT cf. Plutarch, *Dinner of the seven wise men, Mor.* 156A.

1.15 *Tainted* or *corrupt* is found only here and Jude 8 in the NT.

1.16 *Detestable* is used only here in the NT (cf. Prov. 17.15; Ecclus. 41.5) but the cognate noun occurs in Luke 16.15.

Advice about the desired behaviour of ordinary believers
   2.1–10

Titus is exhorted to give particular advice to individual groups of believers, divided according to age, sex and status. I Tim. 5.1–2 had briefly advised Timothy about the kinds of relationship he should develop with older and younger men and women, and I Tim. 6.1–2 had given instructions about the behaviour required of believing slaves. The same groups appear here, but the content of Titus' paraenetic to older and younger men and women is included. The passage is introduced by the reminder that Titus' speech should accord with *sound doctrine* or *healthy teaching*, as in the case of the overseer (1.9). He is to teach *older men* to be *sober* (cf. I Tim. 3.2, 11, of the overseer and wives of deacons) and *temperate, and sound in faith*, like the overseer/elder (1.8–9). *In love and in fortitude* or *endurance* are also combined in the advice about Timothy's own behaviour in I Tim. 6.11 and II Tim. 3.10. These older men, then, are to conform to the character sketches of leaders, who would be chosen from among their number.

2.3–5   *Older women* are exhorted to be *reverent or worthy of reverence in their demeanour*. What this general characterisation implies is then illustrated: *not scandalmongers* is also forbidden deacons' wives in I Tim. 3.11, scandalmongering being a vice frequently associated with women in contemporary literature, although it is also attributed to men in the last days (II Tim. 3.3); *not slaves to excessive drinking* corresponds to the sobriety required of older men (2.2); *teaching what is good* is paraphrased by REB: *they must set a high standard, and so teach*. Their teaching role, however, is confined to instructing younger women, not men (cf. I Tim. 2.12). They are also to be *loving wives and mothers*. Nothing is said about the need for older or younger men to love their wives and children. Moreover, older

99

women are to teach younger women to be *temperate* (cf. 2.2 of older men and 1.8 of the overseer), *chaste* or *pure,* as Timothy is encouraged to be (I Tim. 5.22), *busy at home* or *good managers of the household,* as in the case of remarried widows (I Tim. 5.14), and *respecting the authority of their husbands* or *subordinated to their own husbands,* as in I Tim. 2.12. In other words, women are to be encouraged to conform to the conservative conceptions of the matronly virtues espoused in Hellenistic literature (see the commentary on I Tim. 2.9–15). The advice is justified by a concern not to bring the *teaching of God* (REB paraphrases *the gospel)* into *disrepute,* which conformity to conservative male requirements would avoid. No question is raised about whether non-conformity to worldly wisdom would better express fidelity to God, as Paul argues in I Cor. 1–2.

2.6–8 *Younger men* are also to be encouraged *to be temperate* or *self-controlled,* like older men and younger women (2.2, 4). That Titus is to set them *an example of good conduct* or *works* suggests that he is to be understood as a younger man too, like Timothy (I Tim. 4.12; II Tim. 2.22). Like those epistles, this one offers advice from an older and more experienced man, Paul, to a younger associate, as in Graeco-Roman literature (e.g. Seneca's letters to his nephew). This focus on Titus, however, allows a recital of virtues appropriate to his teaching role: *integrity and seriousness,* the second virtue being required of the overseer who was to teach (I Tim. 3.4). That his teaching should be *healthy* recalls 2.1, but now it is recommended as teaching which is unexceptionable, leaving an opponent with *nothing to say to our discredit. Opponent* could refer to those mentioned in 1.10–16 or to an outsider (cf. I Tim. 3.7).

2.9–10 Last of all, *slaves'* behaviour is considered: *slaves are to be subordinate to their masters in everything* or *in every way.* The absolute authority of masters over slaves is endorsed, regardless of the masters' behaviour or demands (see the commentary on I Tim. 6.1–2). Slaves are to *give satisfaction* to their earthly masters, whereas elsewhere in the NT this demand is made only of people's relation to God. They are *not to answer back,* even in response to a master's immoral demands. Nor are they *to pilfer,* a common complaint against slaves, who might only be able to get enough to eat by taking what had not strictly been allocated to them. That they are to *show all faithfulness and goodness* (REB *be absolutely trustworthy)* is recommended so that *in all this they will add lustre to the teaching of*

God our Saviour. God our Saviour is not understood to save people from the cruelty of slavery, as the God of Exodus is understood to do. This advice shows that, whereas the epistle in general encourages people to express their belief in good and loving actions, that teaching had not been applied to the treatment of slaves. Had such an application been made, believers would have been required to buy the freedom of believing slaves, so that they could live in a manner advocated for all other believers. In this whole section, 2.1–10, Hellenistic ethical teaching is simply adopted and endorsed, without any real attempt at understanding how Christian love might affect social relations, in spite of the theological reflection which follows.

God's grace gives a new life of salvation
2.11–15

2.11–12   The repeated exhortations to perform good works, which the Pastorals contain, do not imply a belief that people are able to save themselves through their performance of good works. On the contrary, it is *God's grace* in Christ Jesus that saves people (cf. II Tim. 1.8–9; Titus 3.4–5). This *grace* is personified as acting in the world, in order to safeguard the sophisticated sense of God's transcendence which the Pastorals express (I Tim. 1.17; 6.15–16; and compare the similar personification of God's *kindness and generosity* in 3.4). REB's *has dawned upon the world with healing for all mankind* paraphrases *appeared for the salvation of mankind*. The emphasis on God's purpose to save *all people* is also found in I Tim. 2.4. Once people have been saved by God's grace, however, their present saved existence is conceived in terms of being *disciplined* or *trained, disciplined* away from old habits and into a new form of life. The use of *we* and *us* reinforces the earlier association of Paul and Titus in a shared faith (1.1). Hellenistic literature also conceives the philosophical life as a period of training (cf. I Tim. 4.7; II Tim. 3.16; Epictetus 2.18.27; 3.3.14; Diodorus Siculus 16.6). What distinguishes the Pastorals, however, is their focus on the prior need of God's grace through Christ Jesus. Hence *renouncing impiety* is essential to the Pastorals, as it was to Philo and Josephus. Also to be renounced are *worldly desires* (cf. II Tim. 2..2; 3.6) as in Hellenistic philosophy. Such renunciation is understood to allow people the cultivation of the essential virtues: *temperance, justice and piety* (cf. Mott 1978; REB interprets *honesty and godliness*). *In the present age* (cf. I Tim. 6.17; II Tim. 4.10) makes it clear that people's lives are to be transformed even before the eschaton, but the eschatological *hope* is also mentioned to encourage people's present transformation. REB's *looking forward to the happy fulfilment of our hope* interprets *looking forward to the blessed hope* (cf. 1.2).

2.13–14   What is to be hoped for is then spelt out: *and the appearing of the splendour of our great God and (of our) Saviour Christ Jesus.* REB renders this: *when the splendour of our great God and Saviour Christ Jesus appear.* This possible translation attributes divinity to Jesus. The more likely translation, however, is: *of our great God and of our Saviour Christ Jesus,* which does not attribute divinity to Jesus. The reasons for suggesting that this is a better translation are that nowhere else in the Pastorals is divinity attributed to Jesus, and in II Tim. 4.1 a distinction between God and Christ Jesus at the eschaton is maintained. Moreover, in I Tim. 2.5, Jesus is specifically called a human being, and elsewhere, the Pastorals contain references and allusions to his death (I Tim. 2.6; 3.16; II Tim. 2.11). The Pastorals emphasise the transcendence of God (I Tim. 1.17; 6.15–16), and this has led to the personification of God's virtues when God's activity in the world is described (Titus 2.11; 3.4). Futhermore, this is what has determined the conception of the human being Jesus as a mediator between God and humanity (I Tim. 2.5). Had the Pastorals presented the human being Jesus as God, it would have been necessary to explain how this could be so, without either denying Jesus' humanity or compromising God's transcendence. It took Christian theologians centuries to find an adequate way of expressing the belief that Christ is one person, both fully human and also God, in the Chalcedonian Definition of 451 CE, and even that definition was rejected by some Christians.

The reference to believers' hope in the future appearing of Christ Jesus leads back into a reflection on what he achieved in his first appearing. *He it is who gave* (REB interprets *sacrificed*) *himself for us* conceives the whole of Jesus' historical life as a self-giving (cf. I Tim. 2.6 and Gal. 1.4; 2.20), a self-giving which served a particular purpose: *to redeem us* (the cognate verb is used in I Tim. 2.6; REB interprets *set us free*). The language of ransoming slaves or war captives intimates the new life which Christ effected, not, however, as an escape from social slavery or captivity but as an escape from the captivity of *all wickedness* or *lawlessness* (cf. Rom. 6.19). It is more usual in other Paulines to present this captivity as captivity to *sin* (e.g. Rom. 3.23–24; I Cor. 15.3; Gal. 1.4; and see I Tim. 1.15), and Romans and Galatians, in particular, contrast the works of the law with justification by faith in pointing up the difference which Christ has brought. In spite of the reference to the circumcision group in 1.10, however, the epistle to Titus makes a more general contrast between human deeds and God's grace. Galatians and Romans are concerned with whether Gentiles who believe in Jesus as God's Messiah should also keep the requirements of the Jewish law and, in effect, become Jews through circumcision and eating kosher food. They deny that necessity and assert that faith in Christ is all that is needed as Gentiles' ground for salvation. The Pastorals take for granted that Gentiles do not need to keep these Jewish requirements, and are concerned to emphasise that God's grace has saved believers for a new life of good works in Christ Jesus. Salvation, then, is understood to be God's gift to believers, not something earned by their good works. But the Pastorals, like other Paulines, insist that this gift from God effects a new form of life in which believers are empowered to perform good deeds. They encourage people who have been saved by God through Christ Jesus to pursue an active life of justice, mercy and love. This teaching is much more pertinent for contemporary Christians than is the more particular concern of Galatians and Romans about the relationship of non-Jewish believers to the Jewish law.

On the other hand, Romans 4–8 and Galatians 4–5 explore the new freedom of believers in terms of sonship, concepts foreign to the Pastorals, despite their occasional references to God as Father and believers as brothers (I Tim. 1.2; 4.6; 5.1; 6.2; II Tim. 1.2; 4.21; Titus 1.4). The words for *free* and *freedom*, like that for *son,* never occur in the Pastorals. This perhaps explains the lack of confidence in ordinary believers which characterises the Pastorals (contrast Phil. 1.3–11; I Thess. 1.2–10; 2.14), and the absence of the image of the church as the body of Christ in contrast to other Paulines (cf. Rom. 12; I Cor. 12). Moreover, other Pauline letters can appeal to the believing community to rectify matters which are criticised (e.g. I Cor. 5.4–5; Gal. 6.1–10), whereas the church structure advocated by the Pastorals is hierarchical and conceived as God's household, a household like that in Graeco-Roman society. Paul's delegates are instructed to put right faults with the help of free, male heads of households.

Nevertheless, Titus 2.14 does briefly characterise the new life for which believers have been redeemed by God through Christ Jesus: *to purify for himself a chosen people* (REB paraphrases *to make us his own people, pure*). Here language about the Jewish people in the Jewish Scriptures is transferred to the Christian community (Ex. 19.5; Deut. 14.2; Ezek 37.23). *Purity* in a moral sense is repeatedly recommended in the Pastorals (cf. I Tim. 1.5; 3.9; II Tim. 1.3; 2.22; Titus 1.15). In other words, God's grace in Christ Jesus is understood to save people, but once they are saved, people are expected to live out their salvation in pure lives, *eager to do good* or *zealous for good works*. God's grace, then, makes possible human performance of good deeds.

2.15 The section ends by reminding Titus of his responsibility to teach (2.1), now defined as *urge* or *encourage* and *convince* or *convict* (REB *argue)*, the positive and negative aspects of the teacher's task. *With all authority* highlights Titus' status as Paul's delegate, in spite of his youth (2.7). *Let no one disregard* or *despise you* similarly offsets tendencies which might be expected in a patriarchal society with regard to a younger man (cf. I Tim. 4.12). Timothy's special status had been explained in terms of his charisma from God, as well as his legitimate representation of Paul (I Tim. 4.14; II Tim. 1.6), but no reference is made to Titus' charisma.

Notes on 2.1–15

Again, this section contains distinctive vocabulary:

2.3 *Demeanour* is used only here in the NT, cf. Plutarch, *Marcellus* 23.6.

Teaching what is good The word is found nowhere else in surviving ancient Greek literature.

2.4 *Loving wives and mothers* is literally *husband-lovers and children-lovers*, words common in Hellenistic literature (e.g. Plutarch, *Advice to bride and groom* 29 and *Dialogue on love* 23, *Mor.* 142A; 769C) but never used elsewhere in the NT, like 2.5 *busy at home;* 2.7 *integrity, none can take exception* (cf. II Macc 4.47) and *opponent* (cf. Diod. L. 1.84), and 2.12 *worldly.*

2.10 *Pilfer* occurs only here and Acts 5.2–3 in the NT, cf. Polybius 10.16.6.

2.15 *These are your themes* is an interpretive addition to the Greek text.

Advice about all believers' relations with the governing authorities and with outsiders
3.1–8a

3.1–3   Once more, the advice is grounded theologically by reflection on the change in people's lives which God is said to have wrought in Christ Jesus. That believers are to be reminded about being *submissive to rulers and authorities* suggests a situation in which the beliefs and expectations of believing communities were not shared by the larger society and its rulers. But both Jewish and Christian writers nevertheless advised their communities to be submissive to pagan authorities, partly as an affirmation that the world is God's, and partly as a recognition that this would be less likely to lead to persecution (cf. Josephus, *War* 4.175; Rom. 13.1–10; I Peter 2.13–17). Moreover, Titus 3.1 further defines *to be submissive* by another verb in apposition: *to obey*, a verb most often used to advocate obedience to God (e.g. Plato, *Apology* 29D; Josephus, *Ant.* 17.159; Acts 5.29). That verb in turn, however, is even further defined: *to be ready for any good work*, a definition which could exclude believers' obedience to any ruler's demand for bad actions. Apostasy, for example, or murder could not be justified by appeal to a ruler's orders. Not many ordinary believers would have had direct contact with ruling authorities, unless they behaved in ways which were taken to be dangerous to state security, but all would have lived among pagan neighbours, and offending them could have led to their complaints reaching rulers. Hence, Titus is also told to remind them to *slander no one, and always to show forbearance and a gentle disposition to all*. Elsewhere, concern is expressed that believers' behaviour should not cause outsiders to slander them (e.g. I Tim. 6.1; Titus 2.5). Here believers are warned against slandering outsiders. Such slandering is attributed to those who teach differently (I Tim. 1.20; 6.4) and to people in the last days (II Tim. 3.2), that is, to people whose bad examples should cause repugnance, not imitation. Moreover, the avoidance of quarrels and the showing of forbearance and gentleness are required of both overseer and Timothy in relation to opponents (I Tim. 3.3; II Tim. 2.25). In other words, leaders are to provide examples which ordinary members could emulate in their relations with outsiders.

3.3   This reference to outsiders leads to a recollection of the former manner of life which Paul and Titus had once shared with them. This former lifestyle, however, is represented in the extreme terms beloved of Hellenistic writings (cf. Eph. 2.1–3). By contrast, II Tim. 1.3, 5 represents Paul's, Timothy's, and their forebears' earlier lives positively. Here, many of the vices listed to characterise the life of unbelievers are used elsewhere in the Pastorals of opponents: *being lost* or *led astray* (cf. II Tim. 3.13), *disobedience* (cf. 1.16), *malice* (cf. I Tim. 6.10; II Tim. 4.14), and *envy* (cf. I Tim. 6.4). *Slaves to passions and pleasures of every kind* expands the reference to *worldly desires* which the new life in Christ Jesus had been said to train believers to renounce (2.12; cf. Epictetus 2.16.45; 2.18.8–9; Philo, *Special Laws* 4.93). The list is summarised: *hateful ourselves, we loathed one another* (cf. Philo, *Decalogue* 131), a picture contrary to the Pastorals' exhortation to love (I Tim. 1.5, 14; 2.15; 4.12; 6.11; II Tim. 1.7, 13; 2.22; 3.10; Titus 2.2, 10). It is noticeable that this list does not include idolatry, as other Pauline lists which describe the life of unbelievers do (e.g. Rom. 1.23; I Cor. 5.10; 6.9). Perhaps the first person form, *we*, led to the exclusion, but it is more likely that this list is taken over from those which describe a life without philosophical reflection in Hellenistic literature, in which idolatry would not feature. The worship of dumb idols was no longer a live issue in this literature. Instead, what is opposed is an inadequate conception of the transcendent God and this God's purpose. Nevertheless, the Pastorals do not suppose, as Hellenistic literature does, that reflection alone can bring about change. Rather, as in 2.11, the change from a vicious to a virtuous life is understood to be accomplished by God.

3.4–8a   Again, the text safeguards the perception of God's transcendence by attributing his activity in the world to his personified virtues: *kindness* or *goodness* (cf. Rom. 2.4) and *generosity* or *love of humanity*. The time *when* these virtues are understood to have *dawned or appeared* is the advent of Jesus Christ, through whom God is conceived as saving people. This is why both God and Jesus can be called *our Saviour* (3.4, 6). Once more, any suggestion that human beings might be able to save themselves through their own good deeds is specifically excluded: *not from works which we did in righteousness* (REB paraphrases more vaguely *not for any good deeds of our own*). On the contrary, *he saved us* is understood as an expression of his *mercy*, made effective *through a washing of rebirth and a renewal of the Holy Spirit, which he lavished upon us through Jesus Christ our Saviour, so that, justified by his grace, we might in hope become heirs of eternal life*. This short section, which I have quoted at length because it is important to notice all the details, is most reminiscent of other Pauline statements, though some of its teaching is distinctive. God's *mercy* is emphasised in Rom. 11.31–32; the only other NT reference to *renewal* occurs in Rom. 12.2 in the expression: 'the renewal of your mind, which is your spiritual worship'; *justified by his grace* is parallel to Rom. 3.24; *heirs* describes believers in Rom. 4.13–14; 8.17; Gal. 3.29; 4.1, 7; *eternal life* is said to be the end to which believers' sanctification tends in Rom. 6.22. On the other hand, *works done by us in righteousness* is without parallel in the NT; *washing* occurs elsewhere only in Eph. 5.26; *regeneration* or *rebirth* in this sense is found nowhere else in the NT; and none of the other Paulines refer to the Holy Spirit as *lavished* or *poured out*, an allusion to Joel 3.1 (Acts 2.17). Moreover, this and II Tim. 1.14 are the only references to *the Holy Spirit* in the Pastorals, although God's sustaining gift of inspiration is mentioned in II Tim. 1.7. Here, the Holy Spirit is represented as God's agent of renewal. Many commentators interpret *washing* as a reference to Christian baptism, both here and in Eph. 5.26. This is possible but uncertain. It is noticeable that the Pauline verb *to baptise* is never used in the Pastorals, and *washing*, like *renewal*, could refer to the moral change which God effects in believers through Jesus Christ and the Holy Spirit, which is the subject of this section (cf. Ps. 51.2; Plutarch, *Mor.* 722D). Certainly, there are no unambiguous references either to the eucharist or to baptism elsewhere in the Pastorals. These epistles, rather, concentrate on exhortation to put belief into practice by performing good deeds through God's empowerment in Christ Jesus. That *this is a saying you can trust* both highlights the importance of the passage and encourages acceptance of its teaching.

A summary of the advice to Titus about the instructions he is to give to ordinary believers and the stand he is to take against opponents.

3.8b–11

3.8b Titus is exhorted to *insist on* the acceptance of the teaching contained in the epistle, in the sense that he is to speak confidently about those matters. *Those who have come to believe in God* are those who have come to believe in the God who saves people in Christ Jesus. These Titus should encourage *to be sure* or *careful to devote themselves to good works* (cf. Prov. 26.17). *Good works* recalls 2.14 and 3.1, and the more detailed elucidations of 2.1–10, which are presented as descriptions of the new life which God has given. REB's *useful to society* interprets *useful to human beings*.

3.9 Moreover, Titus is to *avoid* the kinds of interests espoused by those of the circumcision (1.1–16): *foolish speculations* (cf. I Tim. 6.4; II Tim. 2.23), *genealogies* (cf. I Tim. 1.4), *quarrels* (cf. I Tim. 6.4; Rom. 1.29), *and controversies* (cf. II Tim. 2.23), here defined as *controversies over the law* in line with the depiction of these opponents as the circumcision party. Perhaps, then, *genealogies* should also be understood in terms of a claim to be descendants of Abraham. Since the epistle contains neither a refutation of such a claim nor a positive exposition of the believer's relationship to the Jewish law, however, it is probably better to understand the passage as a conventional denigration of a lifestyle opposed to that which the epistle advocates, a denigration which serves to discourage imitation. The judgment that these interests are *unprofitable and futile* confirms this interpretation.

3.10–11 Not only is Titus to avoid being drawn into speculations and quarrels, but practical advice is given about his behaviour towards any believer who is *contentious or who causes dissensions* (cf. I Cor. 11.19; Gal. 5.20). Titus is to *admonish him once or twice* (REB interprets *he should be allowed a second warning*). This disciplinary responsibility is placed solely in the hands of the Pauline delegate. No encouragement is given to involve even the local elders in the procedure, much less the whole community (contrast I Cor. 5.4; Matt. 18.15–20). A hierarchical church structure is encouraged, but this means that exclusion of a member from the community by the community cannot be a last resort. Rather, Titus is told that he himself is to *have nothing to do with him.* He is to recognise the person who does not heed the warnings as someone *who has a distorted mind* (cf. Gal. 5.20). Such a person is called *self-condemned* for the same reason, but he is also *self*-condemned because the community to which he belongs has not condemned him. Moreover, it is remarkable that no reference is made to God's eschatological judgment nor to the person's forfeiture of eternal life (cf. 1.2–3; 2.13; II Tim. 2.19, 25; 4.14).

Concluding details, greetings and the final grace
3.12–15

3.12   The details include arrangements for Titus to rejoin Paul and exhortation that the local community should support two travelling missionaries. An impression is created of a Pauline group of associates who are mutually devoted and who can expect sustenance from the groups they serve. *Artemas* is mentioned only here in the NT. *Tychicus* is mentioned in Acts 20.4 as an Asian associate of Paul; in Eph. 6.21 as an associate whom Paul would send to take news to Ephesus; in Col. 4.7 as a Pauline associate who would take news to Colossae; and in II Tim. 4.12 as an associate who would travel to Ephesus, presumably to replace Timothy. Here, he or Artemas would be sent to Crete to allow Titus to join Paul at Nicopolis where he plans to spend the winter. In the ancient world, travel was even more difficult during the winter than at other times (cf. II Tim. 4.21; I Cor. 16.6). *Nicopolis*, mentioned only here in the NT, was a common name for Greek cities, but this one is usually identified with that in Epirus, described by Strabo (7.7.3).

3.13–14   In the meantime, Titus is encouraged to do his *utmost to help* other Pauline delegates *on their travels* (cf. I Cor. 16.1). *Zenas the lawyer* is mentioned only here in the NT, but *Apollos* is decribed in I Corinthians as an influential teacher who had worked in Corinth (I Cor. 1.12; 3.4–6, 22; 4.6) and whom Paul had urged to visit that community again (I Cor. 16.12). Acts 18.24 relates that he was a Jew from Alexandria, an eloquent preacher whom Aquila and Priscilla had drawn into the Christian movement at Ephesus, and who had later visited the church in Corinth (Acts 18.24–19.1). It is possible that Zenas and Apollos are understood to be the bearers of the epistle to Titus, and who would need support in order to travel further. Helping them would afford an opportunity for the believers in Crete to perform some of *the good works* recommended by the epistle (cf. 1.8; 3.8). Here the good works are defined as those which meet *urgent needs*. Acts 28.10 uses a similar expression with reference to the Maltese people's support of Paul and his companions for their journey by boat. The epistle insists that only God's grace and benevolence has saved believers in Christ Jesus, but those who are saved are expected to express their new life in a similar benevolence, *not to be unproductive* or *fruitless*.

3.15 Paul's companions are included with him in sending greetings, but none are named (cf. I Cor. 16.19–20; II Cor. 13.12–13). Perhaps some of those already named in 3.12–13 are understood to be included. In any case, Paul is represented as the central figure of a group, not as an isolated teacher. Similarly, the greetings are sent not to Titus alone but to *all who love us in the faith,* that is, to those who remain faithful to the Pauline mission rather than to those criticised in 1.10–15; 3.10–11. As is usual in NT epistles, these conventional greetings are adapted to express the theological beliefs of Christian communities by the final grace: *Grace be with you* (plural). Although the epistle is addressed to Titus alone, and all the other commands are in the second person singular, this final petition includes those whom Titus is to exhort and admonish (cf. I Tim. 6.21; II Tim. 4.22).

Notes on 3.1–15

Again, some of the vocabulary of this section is unique in the NT:

3.3 *Hateful ourselves* (cf. Philo, *Decalogue* 131); 3.8 *be sure* or *careful* (cf. Epictetus 3.24.3); 3.10 *contentious* (cf. Diog. L. 7.126); and 3.11 *self-condemned*.

3.8 *Insist on* is used only in the Pastorals among NT writings (cf. I Tim. 1.7; Plutarch, *Fabius* 14.4; Josephus, *Against Apion* 2.14).

Other words are unique within the epistles attributed to Paul: 3.1 *obey* (cf. Acts 5.29; 27.21; Polybius 3.4.3); 3.3 *pleasures* (cf. Luke 8.14; James 4.3; Philo, *Husbandry* 83–84); 3.4 *generosity or love of humanity* (cf. Acts 28.2, where, however, it refers to human love of humanity; Philo, *Embassy to Gaius* 73); 3.9 *unprofitable* (cf. Heb. 7.18); 3.14 *unproductive* (cf. II Peter 1.8).

Appendix
Who wrote the Pastoral Epistles?

This question arises because of the distinctive features of the three pastoral epistles in comparison to other epistles attributed to Paul. These distinctive features are of different kinds. The first is linguistic and stylistic. The language sometimes echoes other Pauline literature, as in the case of the reference to *those of the circumcision* (Titus 1.10) or in some of the statements of Titus 3.5–7, but even these passages also exhibit special characteristics. So, for example, the Pastorals insist that God's grace, not people's good works, effects salvation, whereas Romans and Galatians make a more particular contrast between justification by faith and works of the Jewish law. Moreover, much of the ethical vocabulary of the Pastorals is unique in the Pauline corpus, some of it even unique in the NT, as the notes have detailed. The emphasis on *piety* and *moderation* or *good judgment* are without parallel in other Paulines, as is the medical metaphor which presents approved teaching as *healthy* and opposing teaching as diseased. Even the introductory thanksgiving of I and II Timothy expresses *I give thanks* in terms which are commonly used in Hellenistic letters rather than those found in other Paulines. And, as Harrison points out in his two studies (1921, 1964), the particles, prepositions and pronouns used in other Paulines, which normally characterise a person's style irrespective of subject matter, are absent from the Pastorals.

Moreover, the style of the Pastorals is less dynamic than that of the other Paulines. Romans, I and II Corinthians, Galatians and Philippians give the impression of an author who has too much to say in too little space, and who is creating new images in which to convey subtle insights in order to meet the immediate needs of particular churches. By contrast, the Pastorals' style is more steady, prosaic and repetitive, designed to convey a more general understanding of the faith, with an emphasis on conservation, the passing on of a deposit, to be treasured in order to meet whatever needs might arise in the churches. 'False' teaching is set beyond the pale by a series of conventional derogatory epithets, rather than being refuted.

The second distinction is theological, christological and soterio-logical. The adoption of Hellenistic epiphany language to refer to Jesus' historical *appearing* as well as his eschatological *appearing*, the term *Sovereign* for God, and the emphasis on God's transcendence which has led both to the personification of his virtues as acting in the world and to the presentation of Jesus as the human *mediator* between God and humanity, draw the Pastorals closer to Philo's writings than to the other Paulines. Moreover, the assertions that Jesus' past appearance *saved* people, in the past tense, so that the present existence of believers can be called *salvation*, is unusual among the Paulines.

The third distinction concerns the structure of local churches approved by the Pastorals. Although they contain occasional references to God's fatherhood and to believers as brothers and sisters, this egalitarian terminology is marginalised in favour of a patriarchal, hierarchical structure of local elders, overseers and deacons, of free male householders, who are to rule over the communities, keeping other believers in obedient subordination, as heads of households were expected to do in the larger society. Gone is the language of freedom and sonship, and gone is the image of the church as the body of Christ in favour of the image of the church as God's patriarchal household. Hence the concern with *elders*, who are not mentioned in other Paulines. Hence, too, the emphasis on women's subordination to their husbands and the encouragement of younger widows to remarry.

There is also another difficulty in attributing the Pastoral Epistles to Paul. Their references to people and places cannot be fitted into a reconstruction of Paul's life and mission based either on the other Paulines or on Acts. Moreover, early attestation to the recognition of the Pastorals is lacking. In the second century CE, Tatian rejected the Pauline authorship of I and II Timothy, and accepted only Titus, which contains stronger similarities to Romans and Galatians. The 'heretic' Marcion rejected all three epistles, although this may be explained by their emphasis on the goodness of God's creation, which he would have found uncongenial. More telling is their apparent absence from the Chester Beatty Papyrus, which is dated about 200 CE. The early churches were well aware of the possibility of forgeries. A writer who wanted his work to appear authoritative could adopt the name of a respected, deceased figure in order to gain a hearing, just as some Hellenistic philosophical writings claim to be written by classical philosophers like Socrates or Plato. In a world in which communication was slow, and in which authentic letters were dictated to professional scribes who could write in a neat, legible hand, it was difficult to distinguish genuine from pseudonymous. The only criteria which could be applied were style, theological 'orthodoxy' and early attestation. The Gnostic Epistle to Rheginos could be rejected on these grounds, but other letters, attributed to Paul, like the epistle to the Laodiceans, III Corinthians, and the correspondence between Paul and Seneca, retained their popularity for centuries, before they were rejected as forgeries, because they were found to be useful. And the Pastoral Epistles would also prove invaluable to third century churches, which were opposing Gnosticism, and which were developing a patriarchal, hierarchical church structure for which the Pastorals seem to give Pauline warrant.

Nevertheless, the Pastoral Epistles clearly claim Pauline authorship, and some contemporary scholars have tried to meet these difficulties and to defend their claim (e.g. Guthrie, 1957; Kelly, 1963; Spicq, 1969; Knight, 1992). The most favoured way of dealing with the impossibility of fitting the Pastorals' personal and geographical references into a recontruction of Paul's life based on the other Paulines or Acts is to suggest that Paul was released from the Roman captivity recorded in Acts 28, that he engaged in further missionary activity in the eastern empire, in spite of his plan to go west (Rom. 15.24, 28), and that II Timothy refers to a second Roman imprisonment which ended in his martyrdom. This would also allow a period during which Pauline teaching could have developed. There is, however, no external evidence to support the hypothesis of Paul's second imprisonment at Rome, and Acts, although it does not relate Paul's martyrdom in chapter 28, does seem to imply it (Acts 20.23–24, 36–38; 21.4–5, 10–14).

Given the slight possibility that Paul lived for a considerable time after his composition of the other Paulines, however, can the distinctive teachings of the Pastorals, in their vocabulary and style, their theology, christology, soteriology, ethics and church organisation, be understood as coherent developments of earlier Pauline teaching? There are two major obstacles to accepting that they can. The Pastorals' style and vocabulary represent a higher form of Hellenistic Greek than that of the other Paulines or of most of the

115

other NT writings. They are closer to Acts than to the other Pauline epistles. The author clearly had a privileged Hellenistic education, like that of Epictetus, Plutarch or Dio Chrysostom, or like that of the Jewish Hellenistic writers, Philo and Josephus. Hence, the author can draw on Hellenistic traditions for metaphors and ethical exhortation. The Pastorals try to integrate this teaching into their theological and christological belief structure, but sometimes Hellenistic teaching seems to be taken over wholesale, as obviously wise (e.g. I Tim. 6.6–8), without any real attempt at integration, or, in the case of the advocacy of free, male leadership, without any fundamental examination of its presuppositions. We would have to suppose that Paul, after writing his other letters, engaged in a period of concentrated study of Hellenistic literature, and that this study occasioned the changes. Knight (1992) suggests that his conversations with Luke, who is taken to be the author of Acts, might have influenced him. But, apart from the uncertainty about the authorship of Luke–Acts, what is needed to explain the distinctive characteristics of the Pastorals, which differ from those of Acts in some respects (see Harrison, 1921, 1964), is a sustained and rigorous study of Hellenistic literature, which would require both the desire and the leisure.

Another explanation for some of the changes, proposed by Guthrie (1957) and taken up by Knight (1992), for example, is that the Pastoral Epistles are distinctive because they are addressed to Pauline associates rather than to whole communities. This is said to explain the lack of engagement with and refutation of opposing teachings, since Timothy and Titus might be expected to be already well acquainted with Paul's refutations. But this raises a second major difficulty. If Timothy and Titus were so well versed in the complex arguments of Paul's refutations that they would need no further help, why would they need to be instructed about the more mundane matters which form the content of the Pastorals? Moreover, if we ask what they would have known about Paul's teaching, from references to them in other Paulines, we gather that they were familiar with the church at Corinth. Then why do the Pastorals never explain, never even refer to, his changing his earlier teaching about the nature of the church and its leadership, about the celibacy of women as well as men, and about soteriology? The Pastorals create the impression, not just that they are developing Pauline theology, christology and soteriology, but that they are replacing the earlier versions.

116

For these reasons, most contemporary scholars argue that the Pastorals are pseudonymous, written in the name of Paul, but not written by Paul. Nevertheless, some have made suggestions that would retain a link between the Pastorals and Paul. Harrison (1921, 1964) and Barrett (1963), for example, have suggested that the personal and geographical references in II Tim. 1.16–18; 3.10–11; chapter 4; and Titus 3.12–15 preserve fragments of genuine Pauline letters which have been used as the basis for the Pastoral Epistles. They argue that these sections exhibit the style and vocabulary of parallels in other Paulines, although this is disputed by Cook (1963). But their main reason for making this suggestion is that, otherwise, these sections would seem to fulfil no reasonable purpose in pseud-epigraphical literature. Donelson (1986), however, has shown that such references are found in other clearly pseudonymous letters, like those of Socrates and the Socratics (see A. J. Malherbe, *The Cynic Epistles*, 1977, for an English translation), and that they serve two important functions. First, they create the impression that the pseudonymous epistle is genuine, and, second, they help to depict Paul as the leader of a mutually supportive group of associates who could rely on each other to practise the teaching which the epistle advocates. Fiore (1986) has also argued that this helps to explain the existence of three Pastoral Epistles rather than one.

Another suggestion takes account of Paul's habit of dictating his letters. Perhaps, in the case of the three Pastorals, Paul gave more freedom to his secretary, providing only an outline, and leaving the secretary to express the instructions in his own words (e.g. Jeremias 1975). But this suggestion only causes a further problem. Why is no one else associated with Paul in the opening greetings or at the end, if the secretary played such a formative role in the composition? In any case, if the Pastorals were actually written by someone other than Paul, even on the basis of a sketch, then they are pseudonymous not Pauline.

There is, however, a brief reference to a companion of Paul at the end of II Timothy: *only Luke is with me* (4.11). This has prompted the suggestion that Luke has influenced the style of the Pastorals, either through conversation with Paul or by acting as his unrestrained amenuensis. Identifying this Luke as the author of Luke–Acts is problematic, but readers of the commentary will have noticed some links between the Pastorals and those narratives. Wilson's study (1979) is the most thorough attempt to argue that the author of Luke–Acts later wrote the Pastorals. This thesis, however, is not wholly persuasive. The Pastorals' personal and geopraphical references cannot be fitted into Acts' narrative, as noted already, and Wilson has to adopt Harrison's suggestion that these sections represent genuine Pauline fragments in order to explain the discrepancies. But, if they do, why did their use not lead to a second, revised edition of Acts? Acts, for example, never mentions Titus, nor a Pauline mission on the island of Crete, in spite of the mention of Crete in Acts 27.7. Moreover, Acts never refers to Paul's practice of writing letters and seems to be ignorant of the existence and contents of such epistles, whereas the Pastorals share their genre and echo some of their teachings. We would have to suppose that the author came across Pauline correspondence after completion of Acts, but again, why was a second edition of Acts not circulated? Also, if the author of Acts wanted to pass off the Pastorals as Pauline, why did he not extend Acts to suggest Paul's release from prison? Furthermore, the acceptance of both the Gospel according to Luke and the Acts of the Apostles by churches would have made recourse to pseudonymity unnecessary. Again, the Pastorals present Paul as *the* apostle whose authority has eclipsed that of the other apostles. But Acts refers to Paul as an apostle, along with Barnabas, only in 14.14. For these reasons, it seems better to acknowledge that there are some similarities between Acts and the Pastorals, but that there are also differences, as Harrison argues. The similarities are best explained by the suggestion that the two authors shared the same kind of Hellenistic education.

Scholars like Houlden and Hanson, who argue that the Pastorals are pseudonymous, have tried to ease the problem of their claim to Pauline authorship by proposing that they were written by a disciple of Paul whose admiration of and indebtedness to the great apostle has led him to efface his own contribution. They even suppose that such a practice would have been openly acknowledged, and would have deceived no one. But Donelson is right to protest both that, if the Pastorals are pseudonymous, they did deceive the churches who accepted them into the canon, and that, from our knowledge of the early churches, there seems to have been a consistent policy of rejecting works perceived as pseudonymous, even if it sometimes took a long time to recognise them as such. But Donelson's own explanation of the Pastorals' pseudonymity, in terms of the accepted Greek convention of 'the good lie,' sits uneasily with the Pastorals' explicit teaching, which countenances no good lies. It is their condemnation of the insincerity and falsehoods of others which prompts the accusation of contradiction against this author, if he falsely claims the epistles to be by Paul. How could an author express such clear criticisms while misleadingly attributing his writings to Paul? The answer, however, is not hard to find. Most of us contradict ourselves without noticing. Moreover, the Hellenistic Socratic epistles also espouse a love of truth while claiming to be written by Socrates and his associates. The overwhelming desire to promulgate works which carry the authority of great and respected teachers, in spite of their being later developments, can easily blind authors to the contradiction involved. But should those of us who regard the Pastorals as pseudonymous, and who therefore recognise the contradiction, demand that they be deleted from the canon? This seems hardly necessary. The acceptance of the Pastoral Epistles into the canon did not rest on the belief of their Pauline authorship alone. It also reflects the judgment that these epistles shared the 'orthodoxy' of second, third and fourth century churches, and helped to justify their own interests in apostolic succession and church order.